Three Major Plays:

TATTOOS   SCHOOL PLAY   TYRANNOS

William Young

Table of Contents

Tattoos

A Play in Two Acts

Characters

Julie, sixteen, Anglo, high school student
Wylie, seventeen, Anglo, high school student
Wyman, forty-five, Anglo, Wylie's father, former Army officer

The action takes place in Los Angeles.

Act One

An L.A. suburb, 2001. Julie and Wylie are sitting in patio chairs outside of Starbucks, which appears in the background, stage right. There is big picture window. This room will later be Wylie's bedroom, and at the end of the play a tattoo parlor. The picture window is also used as a screen to project butterfly images and, in scene 8, the movie *Titanic*.

Julie, a Catholic schoolgirl, wears a short, blue-and-green plaid skirt, a white blouse, and low-cut blue Converse All-Stars. Wylie, who is skinny, wears black slacks, a black tank top, black sandals, and a black Starbucks cap with its green insignia. He has long, straight black hair. They are smart, outsider kids.

JULIE

You off?

WYLIE (removing his cap)

I am now. (Setting cap on table) You just hanging out?

JULIE

Yeah. I love Starbucks.

(Julie puts her feet up on another chair, revealing a tattoo on her ankle.)

WYLIE

I like your tattoo.

JULIE

The most girlie tattoo you could imagine.

5

WYLIE

It's cool. I want to get a shield that goes all the way over my shoulders and along my delts. But no wings. The whole wings thing has been done.

JULIE

I want to get another. But I want to be a teacher.

WYLIE (earnestly)

Draw it yourself. Take two or three years to think about it before you go ahead. Make sure it's something that touches you deeply in your soul and you won't be sick of it in a few years. And invest in a professional designer. Pay the extra two or three hundred to get it done right, professionally. Be careful about colors. Go in for slate and gray. Colors fade after a few years, or turn that sickly green-ish color. Slate and gray keeps a classic look. Don't go in for too much shading. Shading will fade and that cool arm and fist will look like a hand in a horror movie emerging from a cloak.

JULIE

I want to get scissors.

WYLIE (skeptical)

You want to make sure it will mean something to you ten, twenty years from now.

JULIE

It means something. I'm a hair stylist. I've been cutting hair since I was ten years old.

WYLIE

Those will have to be some really cool scissors. (Then thinking) Where would you put them?

JULIE (smiling)

Can you guess?

WYLIE

Dude, you'll surely scare the guys away!

(She laughs.)

JULIE

My parents would kill me. They let me get this one (she raises her leg) because I agreed to never get another. "Forever. For life," my dad said. My mother had one, just above her butt. An old school trampstamp. She got it when...

WYLIE

Your dad touches it in the dark.

JULIE

Gross, I know. But it's kind of cool, too. (She lowers her leg.) I heard you're a musician.

WYLIE

Electric guitar.

JULIE

Cool. U2? Remember that party at Skylar's?

WYLIE

Oh, is that her name? Not U2. Grunge. Neil Young. Old school.

JULIE

Really. I love Neil Young. All those oldsters.

WYLIE

I have a turntable. A bunch of LP's.

JULIE

Could I maybe see your room?

(She lights up a cigarette. Offers him one.)

Fag?

WYLIE

I don't smoke. Nor drink.

JULIE

So ungrunge. Straightedge. (She puffs on her cigarette.) Well?

WYLIE

You mean my bedroom?

JULIE

I'm curious. Boy's rooms. I always wanted a brother. Or a sister for that matter. Seriously, I was always inventing an alternate family.

WYLIE

When I left it was messy. Except the bed. Military corners. I doubt my dad cleaned up.

JULIE

Dad, not Mom?

WYLIE

Yeah, Dad.

JULIE (sensing a touchy subject)

Mine are Catholic corners, I guess. (snubs out cigarette) Have you ever heard of a Catholic family with only one child?

WYLIE

Do you like St. Anne's?

JULIE

It's okay. Makes my parents happy. And prayers use up an hour of the school day.
I've known some of the kids since elementary. Like Skylar. Eerie.

WYLIE

I moved around a lot.

JULIE

Why did you graduate Chatsworth early?

WYLIE (impassioned)

I wanted to get out into the real world. Your Catholic school sounds...too clois-
tered. But public school is just too lax for my taste–too...amorphous. My dad was
raised Catholic. My mom–she lives in Maine–is atheist, she says.

JULIE

My parents are strict. ...What does that mean, *amorphous*? "Amor" like love.

WYLIE

Formless. Like morph, but not.

JULIE (laughing)

Like morphine.

WYLIE (serious)

I think that has a different root.

JULIE

Greek, to me.

WYLIE

Did you have to take Latin?

JULIE

No, just catechism. I've picked up a little Latin of course. Especially the dirty parts. Like, *Magna cum laude.* And *summa cum laude.*

>(Wylie, not sure what to make of her, fidgets
>with his cap)

WYLIE

I took German. My dad does two crossword puzzles everyday. He's a wiz. Helps fill his day, I guess. Now that he was retired.

JULIE

From?

WYLIE

Army. That's the military corners. A bed you can bounce a quarter off of.

JULIE

Tell me more.

WYLIE (a bit annoyed)

About him? You'll meet him soon enough... if you come over.

JULIE (you brought him up)

You brought him up.

WYLIE

Did I? What about yours?

JULIE

My dad is a carpenter. My mother a nurse. It's what's called "humble origins." (She picks up his cap.) So that was an invitation?

WYLIE

Sure. ...But fair warning, he's always home. Usually on the computer.

> (She hands his cap to him. He puts it on her.)

I rode my bike.

JULIE

I'll ride on the handlebars. We'll pretend it's middle school. Ancient history!

WYLIE

History is my thing.

> (Wylie stoops to unlock the silver chain on his bike. He steadies the bike. Julie hops on the handlebars.)

What's yours?

JULIE

My thing? Not sure I have one. Maybe theatre. Or used to be. In my youth!

WYLIE

Hold on! (He prepares to pedal.) It's lucky you're so small.

JULIE

Yeah. Seriously. I just fit.

> (Lights down)

Scene Two

Lights up stage left, where Wyman is in the kitchen of his house, sitting at a table drinking beer and working a crossword puzzle. He is a built, middle-aged suave fellow, his hair cut short. A refrigerator sits near the sink. There is a door at the back of the kitchen.

WYMAN

Balls! Sixteen across. I must be getting dumber.

(He tosses aside the newspaper and picks up a book. He starts reading. Lights fade to Wylie's bedroom, stage right.)

(Wylie takes off his Starbucks shirt—he has a white t-shirt underneath—and hangs it up in the closet, at rear. Julie stands there a bit awkwardly as he, next, tries to straighten up a little, picking up clothes off the floor. His room is rather dark, has a kind of medieval or Ming Dynasty lacquered quality to it. A 14th century Scottish broad sword hangs on the wall. There's a desk and chair. A single bed. An electric guitar sits in a corner. The door is left open.)

JULIE

He seemed nice.

WYLIE (tossing a pair of jeans toward the closet)

He's nice to girls.

JULIE

Oh really.

(She sits down on the high bed.)

JULIE

Is that sword real?

WYLIE

You mean *authentic*?

JULIE

Okay. …As in morph.

WYLIE (in his own world)

It's from the 14th Century. Scottish. I got it for my graduation present.

JULIE

I wonder what I'll ask for? (Teasingly) I've got two years to plan it out like my tattoo.

WYLIE (nonresponsive)

I wanted that sword since I was twelve. I'll keep it my whole life.

JULIE

It's beautiful. Can I feel it? (Corrects herself) *Heft* it?

(Wyman enters.)

WYMAN

I bought him that.

WYLIE

Mom, too.

WYMAN

He likes to...quibble.

WYLIE

And?

WYMAN

I just wanted to tell you that Starbucks called, Wylie, and they want you to come in tomorrow. You should give them your cell.

WYLIE

They have it.

WYMAN

That's all I wanted to say.

(But he hesitates.)

What's that tattoo?

JULIE (raising her leg)

See.

WYMAN

Oh. How lovely. Is it permanent?

WYLIE (slightly sarcastic)

No, it's computer generated, sir.

(Julie is a bit taken aback by Wylie's tone. But is even more surprised when Wyman takes a hold of her ankle.)

WYMAN (charmingly)

Like forever? Not "Time's Fool"?

(He lets go of ankle. She is a bit embarrassed.)

JULIE (to Wylie)

I see where you get your love for words.

WYMAN

And tattoos. Anyway, later, you two. Remember, Wylie, Starbucks.

(He exits, closing the door.)

JULIE (looking at the door)

That was nice of him, giving us privacy.

WYLIE

He doesn't allow locked doors.

JULIE (jokingly)

Are we allowed to cuss?

WYLIE (smiling)

No.

JULIE

But it's still nice.

WYLIE

Right, he's nice.

JULIE

To girls.

WYLIE

Right. Especially when he's had a few. A real charmer. Or should I say player.

(Julie stands up.)

JULIE (seeing he's upset, solicitous)

Tell me about the sword.

WYLIE

You wanted to hold it?

JULIE

Is it heavy?

WYLIE

When I first tried it at an antique shop, I couldn't even lift it. My dad had to. Now I can with one hand.

(Wylie takes the sword off the wall. And then holds it out in front of him with one hand.)

But they used two hands.

(He holds the handle with two hands.)

JULIE

It's frightening.

WYLIE

Are you frightened?

JULIE

In five years they didn't sell it?

WYLIE

I spent five years worrying.

JULIE

Did the price go down?

WYLIE

Up. Every year it was a little more out of reach.

JULIE

But now you have it. Forever, yeah?

WYLIE

I hope so. Here, I'll show you.

> (He stands behind her and puts the sword in her hands. The weight surprises her.)

JULIE

Whoa. Seriously, all I need is chainmail and I'm ready for action.

WYLIE

Chainmail is not as heavy as some think.

JULIE

No? (She hands back the sword.) I still have my doll's house. When I was young I liked being able to invest dolls with emotions.

> WYLIE (handing up the sword on the wall)

It's not a play thing.

JULIE

Yes, sir.

> (She notices his displeasure and so goes over to his guitar.)

A sick guitar.

WYLIE (proudly)

I bought it out of my Starbucks' money. Before I only had an acoustic. It's in the closet. This is a vintage Strat.

JULIE

Far out. Play for me, Wylie.

WYLIE (coy)

Moi?

JULIE

Pretty please?

(She sits back down on his bed, tosses off her tennis shoes, and crosses her legs. He tunes his guitar. He picks out a few chords.)

Dude!

WYLIE

What do you want to hear?

JULIE

Surprise me.

WYMAN

Okay.

(He picks out a tune, and then starts to play. As he plays, she stands up on the bed and starts to dance. She takes off her top. She's braless. She takes off her skirt. She is wearing only panties. Looks at the door.)

JULIE

Lock it?

(But, though looking at her, he doesn't respond–as if he is in a trance, transported
somewhere. He stands next to her and continues to wail on his guitar, as if tattooing
her. Butterfly tattoos appear all over her
body, via lighting.)

(Sound diminishes and light fades, shifting
to Wyman. He stands at the refrigerator,
back to us. Opens it and grabs a beer. Twists
off the top. Drinks.)

Scene Three

Julie half opens the backdoor, which leads to the kitchen of Wyman and Wylie's
house. She is in her Catholic school outfit. Wyman stands at the stove, stirring
a pot. He's dressed casually, in shorts. He is also drinking beer. A newspaper is
spread out on the kitchen table.

JULIE

Wylie?

WYMAN

It's Wyman.

JULIE

Oh, sorry, is your...

WYMAN

Son?

JULIE

He wasn't at Starbucks.

WYMAN

Beats me. Come in and wait for him if you like. He's usually here for dinner. I'm cooking.

(She enters.)

JULIE (jokingly)

What's for dinner?

WYMAN

Spaghetti. I have a limited repertoire. A basic mess-hall cook.

JULIE

Your wife doesn't cook?

WYMAN

No wife. She's gone. We're divorced.

JULIE

Oh, my bad. Wylie didn't say. I thought when he said she helped to pay for the sword...

WYMAN

She's been gone since he was twelve. Five years. She lives across the country. Maine. Couldn't live farther away and still be in the continental U.S.! (He drinks.) It's hard on Wylie, I think.

JULIE (a little wary and about to leave)

Will you tell him I stopped by?

WYMAN

If you want me to.

JULIE (looks at him)

Can...may I ask you something?

WYMAN

Please sit. (raising his beer) You?

(Julie sits down at the kitchen table.)

JULIE

Should I?

WYMAN

Well, I'm not your commander.

JULIE

In that case, thanks.

WYMAN

Glass?

JULIE (stretching like a cat)

Please. I love beer.

WYMAN (jokingly)

You're of age, right?

(Having procured the beers, he sits with her at the table. He folds up the newspaper.)

I don't trust that fellow Bush. He didn't even fulfill his National Guard service. Daddy got him good time.

JULIE

I hate *these* uniforms.

WYMAN

They're cute.

JULIE

Not. At least not everyday.

WYMAN

I'm career army. Retired. Three years. Wylie told you, I suppose. I wore a uniform every work day for twenty-five years. Joined right out of high school. I've been all over the world. France. The Mideast. The Philippines. Now I have nothing to do but play on the computer. And cook! I didn't plan ahead. It was always so far off. Like a distant island. I should have known better. I'd been around. Would like to see Wylie go to college. Music is no career.

JULIE

He's good.

WYMAN

Yes, but a man's got to make a living. Starbucks is no career either. Wylie says he hates the Starbucks uniform, but I see he takes good care of it. That's what happens when you grow up on base, I guess. A love/ hate thing. You kids all dress in uniforms anyway, if you ask me. I guess our generation did too. Long hair. But I was in the Army before my generation started. (He drinks.) But you wanted to ask me something?

> (He finishes off his beer and sets it on the table.)

JULIE

Oh, that's okay.

WYMAN

No, go ahead. Wylie may be a while.

> (He goes to the refrigerator. Grabs another
> beer and turns to her.)

You good?

JULIE

Yeah.

WYMAN

So?

JULIE

What I wanted to ask was, so you like like tattoos, sir? Sounds stupid now.

WYMAN

Girls. (He drinks.) They look nice on girls, not so nice on women, in my opinion.

JULIE

May I ask....

WYMAN

Go ahead. I've stood on ceremony long enough.

JULIE

Your wife had one?

WYMAN

My Ex? That was before her time. She wasn't a sailor. She was a prep school girl. East coast. WASP. Very exotic, at least to me. But when you marry them they don't tell you they just want to get back home—and be near their mothers. But they do. She was a good sport for a while, I guess.

JULIE

Me, a Catholic school girl. Once I leave I won't look back.

WYMAN

Catholics have moxie, it's true. They like the rough and tumble. And will cut you up if you cross them!

(She laughs.)

JULIE

So, you neither, no tattoo?

WYMAN (drifting off)

I wasn't a sailor either. They were our transport to the front.

JULIE

My mom has one.

WYMAN (as if returning to familiar things)

Oh, where?

JULIE (hesitating, then...)

Above her rear...

WYMAN

End?

JULIE

Yes, rearend. Ass.

(She laughs.)

WYMAN

What is it?

JULIE

A snowflake.

WYMAN (choking on beer, then...)

What? And she's white?

JULIE (laughing)

Pale Irish last time I checked. I haven't seen it though.

WYMAN

Probably no one has if she's white. Each one is different, they say.

JULIE

You mean snowflakes?

WYMAN

Yeah.

JULIE

I want to be more exotic, myself.

WYMAN

No problem. Just move to a southern continent. You'll stick out like a sore thumb.

JULIE

Thanks for that.

(They laugh. But Wylie stands at the door
leading from the living room to the kitchen.
He holds his sword.)

JULIE

Hi. What's that for? The salad?

WYLIE (not amused)

Can I borrow you for a minute?

JULIE (now standing, but apprehensive)

I was waiting for you.

WYMAN

Don't worry. He takes it down randomly. Are you off today?

WYLIE

I quit. (Then to Julie) Are you coming?

JULIE

Of course.

WYMAN

You what? Quit? Not that you can't do better. (To Julie) I've saved up for his college for a long time...ever since he was born.

JULIE (sitting, then to Wylie)

You're so lucky for that, Wylie.

WYLIE

Yeah, but I'm not going to college.

WYMAN

Why not, for God's sake?

WYLIE (turning away)

I'll be in my room.

(He exits. Wyman and Julie remain sitting at the table.)

JULIE (rising)

Excuse me, sir.

(She exits.)

Scene Four

The livingroom, center stage. Wyman is on the couch watching tv. A beer sits on a side table. He holds the remote in his hand and is flipping through channels. Wylie enters from his room.

WYMAN

I thought the Lakers were on tonight.

WYLIE

ESPN 2, not 1, sir.

WYMAN

ESP too?

WYLIE (playing along)

Wait, Kobe just dunked on Duncan.

WYMAN

You are good. A wizard, I always knew it.

WYLIE

I was watching it in my room.

WYMAN

Don't ruin it. (He drinks.) I thought you liked football? All that strategy.

WYLIE

It's basketball season.

WYMAN

You never went to any kind of high school game, as I recall.

WYLIE

Unlike you?

WYMAN (a bit riled)

And?

WYLIE (backing off)

I wasn't saying anything.

WYMAN

So I like high school sports. It's purer. I despise those professionals. Big money ruined everything. Sports, politics, movies, business, religion, the Armed Forces, you name it. Except maybe education. Isn't that a lark? The only thing untouched by big money is education. Or relatively untouched. You like Kobe Bryant?

(He drinks.)

WYLIE

Sir, I have something to announce.

WYMAN (looking up from tv)

Announce?

WYLIE

Yes, sir. I enlisted, sir.

WYMAN

You what? (Throws remote aside) Is that why you quit Starbucks? What the hell, Wylie? The service? You enlisted? What the hell for? Have you lost your mind? Don't you know this guy Bush is not to be trusted?

WYLIE

I need to support her, of course.

WYMAN

Her? You mean, Julie?

WYLIE

Of course Julie.

WYMAN

What, "of course." It's been two weeks. A fortnight! You just met. She's a darling girl–I can see that–but you two scarcely know each other. You're just kids, for Christ's sake!

WYLIE

Don't you want to know what branch? It's Army, Dad.

WYMAN (rising)

I don't care if it's the Royal Canadian Mounties. Is this to get back at me or something? To challenge me? It's not going to stand, I'll tell you that right now.

WYLIE

I thought you might be proud. It's not like I've never shown any interest–you are the one who first gave me war histories. Julie and I talked it over. She said it was up to me. Didn't you suspect?

WYMAN

Suspect? Me? What? (He thinks) You mean, you've fucking proposed? You've got to be kidding, Wylie? You've never done anything remotely spontaneous and this is no time to start. What is up with you?

WYLIE

What's up with that? I was waiting for an opportunity. I want to get out into the world. Be somebody. (More quietly) She hasn't given me a definite "Yes."

WYMAN

Give me a break. This is just selfish. You're just thinking about yourself, Wylie. Were you going to inform your mother after the fact? I don't get it.

WYLIE

My mother? As if you're concerned about her. Anyway, sir, Julie's on her way over here right now. And now I've got something to offer her.

(Julie knocks at screen door to kitchen.)

WYMAN (sardonic)

Does she know that? Your signing up, Mr. Big Shot?

WYLIE

I texted her. She was supposed to be here earlier.

(Another knock)

Coming. Coming. You know, it would be nice once and a while if you weren't here.

(Wylie starts toward kitchen, but Wyman, beer in hand, pushes him back.)

WYMAN

I'll get it.

(Wylie sits on the arm of the couch.)

WYLIE (calling, apprehensive)

Dad.

(Wyman ignores Wylie. Wyman opens the kitchen door. Julie is out of uniform. She wears jeans and a tanktop.)

WYMAN (still angry)

Come in, Julie. I think he's expecting you, like an expectant mother. And you—you're full of surprises, too.

(She enters. She notices his beer.)

JULIE

Yes, I've come to give Wylie my answer.

WYMAN

So I've been led to believe—or is it, make believe?

JULIE

Are you mad?

WYMAN

I'm...concerned. Let's call it that. Surely your parents won't stand for it.

(Wylie enters kitchen.)

WYLIE (ignoring Wyman, to Julie)

Hi.

JULIE

Hey. Sorry I'm late. (To Wyman) I was going to say "No."

WYLIE

You were? But I've enlisted!

WYMAN

Good choice, Julie. Nothing against you, Wylie. But you kids aren't ready. Not by a long shot. You have no idea. This isn't a video game you're playing.

WYLIE

You should know since you use the computer for other purposes.

JULIE

Wylie!

WYMAN (not reacting to Wylie)

You're not pregnant?

JULIE

Oh my gosh, I'm not...sir. We've hooked up only these weeks. (She thinks.) You don't mean by someone else?

WYMAN

No. Just making sure. Sorry. You two should take your time. Just enjoy it. I'm not too old to remember. You don't know what you have. (Then to Wylie) Don't you think you should have asked me first before going off half-cocked? You need my permission anyway. At seventeen, you're still a minor.

WYLIE

I didn't have her final answer. I joined on faith. (ruefully) Looks like it might be a good place for me anyway, now.

WYMAN

Just because she isn't ready? If you've ever cooked an egg...

JULIE

But I've decided "Yes," I'm ready, totally. Now that I'm here, I'm sure of it. Funny, isn't it?

WYLIE

Really? Really, Julie? (He sits.) God, I'm totally stoked.

WYMAN (incredulous)

But you can't say "Yes." You're not even legal.

JULIE

Yeah, my dad will freak. He wears the pants in the family. (She leans against the refrigerator.) It will be up to him.

WYMAN

Well, I wouldn't hold my breath if I were you. I'm sure you're still his little girl and rightfully so. Nor do you have my permission to marry my son.

JULIE

He'll kick me out of the house probably. Seriously, I'm not naive. But I could maybe stay with a friend, maybe Ashley, until Wylie can come for me. (to Wylie) Three months?

WYLIE

About.

(Wyman finishes his beer and sets it on the table where Wylie remains seated.)

WYMAN

I don't think you kids are listening to me. Look, if you just want to have sex–safe sex–have it. You can have it right here, door locked–though I'll deny it if anyone asks. Or you could do it in a car like normal kids. Like I had to do. You know you can't stay here, Julie? It's nothing against you. It just wouldn't be...seemly. And I'm not about to come between you and your parents.

WYLIE

I hadn't thought of it. But couldn't she? I mean, what other choice is there?

JULIE

I won't be in your way, sir.

> (He goes to the refrigerator–she moves
> out of the way–and procures another beer,
> opens it at the counter, and then turns
> around to look at her.)

WYMAN

I'm saying "No." I can't believe Wylie would want that. But ask your father. It's his call, should he ever speak to you again. (He looks out the window.) I'm not going to have you out in the cold, though. If it comes to it, you can stay in Wylie's room, provisionally, until you can make other arrangements. (Then to her) But I still don't approve. Nor would the Church, should any-one ask.

WYLIE

Thanks, sir. You sure it will be alright? It *would* be convenient.

WYMAN

Convenience is a bad bargain, someone said. The real solution is to not get mar-ried (to Julie) You're a junior, right? You need to finish school.

JULIE

Yes. On the Honor Roll. And I want to graduate. I want to be a teacher. Don't worry. I'll do my homework.

(She laughs, realizing how odd it sounds. Then more serious. Wylie watches them.)

WYMAN

Just get engaged, if you must. There's no need to rush into marriage. Talk to your parents, Julie, your father.

WYLIE

I could hardly have her stay here if we were only engaged, Dad.

WYMAN

If you're only engaged, then maybe her father wouldn't kick her out.

JULIE

Trust me, he would. I would so appreciate it, Mr...

(Wyman sits.)

WYMAN

Just "Wyman." If you stay here—I say, "if," provisionally—you can't be calling me "Mr."

JULIE

Okay...Wyman.

(Wylie stands.)

Wyman and Wylie. Whose idea was that?

WYMAN

His mother's.

WYLIE

Come, Julie.

(Wylie and Julie exit to his bedroom. Wyman
sits down at the table. Opens the newspaper.
Closes it. Stares off.)

Scene Five

Wyman's kitchen, a couple of days later. Julie enters with a suitcase in her hand.
Wyman is cooking. Both stand during the scene.

JULIE

Hi. Wylie here?

WYMAN

Induction. He'll be back for dinner. I see you've got a few belongings.

JULIE

I mean please, he won't even discuss it. Told me not to come home until I came
to my senses.

WYMAN

Where did you say you'd be?

JULIE

I told him you were married–and I gave him your phone number. ... Wasn't easy
deciding what to take with me. I left the dolls.

WYMAN

You might want them, but it's too late now. I suppose you should set it down.

JULIE

Where?

WYMAN

My room down the hall. Wylie sees your suitcase, he's likely to think it's a fait accompli.

JULIE

I take French, too.

WYMAN

Oh, really. Well, first door to the droit.

(Julie exits and returns.)

JULIE

A waterbed. That's so seventies.

WYMAN

How would you know?

JULIE

"That 70's Show." On TV.

WYMAN

Don't know it.

(Wyman stirs the pot.)

You can cook?

JULIE

Well, I'm a hair stylist? I do make-up? ...Spaghetti again?

(Julie goes over to the stove and takes a spoon with the intention of trying the sauce.)

May I?

WYMAN

Be my guest.

(She tries it.)

Well?

JULIE (teasingly)

Not totally gross. Is it better the next day?

WYMAN

Oh, another critic. Can't cook but...woman are nothing if not critical. Like Iago. But don't be fooled. Criticism only makes me stronger.

JULIE

I *can* clean.

WYMAN

As you go.

JULIE (archly)

After I go?

WYMAN

I'm all for personal hygiene. But your job would be homework not housework here.

(Wyman goes to the refrigerator, takes out a
beer, and opens it.)

You know, maybe Wylie should talk to your dad? I mean, I could, but I don't
want to undermine Wylie. Or your father for that matter.

JULIE

Dude, sword, shotgun? I don't think so.

WYMAN

He'd be using the shotgun for just the opposite if you were pregnant.

JULIE

Maybe that's the answer?

WYMAN

I already feel complicit. (Standing at the stove, he drinks.) When Wylie was little,
at bedtime I'd say to him, "Wylie, roger and out." "Sir, roger and out," he'd say.
We were close. Things changed after the divorce.

JULIE

Why didn't he go with her?

WYMAN

Well, he did for six months, when I was in Kuwait. But he missed his buddies
and came back when I came back. But when I moved here, to California, he had
to leave them anyway. He hasn't fit in here so well.

JULIE

Why's that?

WYMAN

Well, he's not use to going to school off base, I guess.

JULIE

Off base! Ha. What does complicit mean, anyway? (lifting the newspaper on the table) I guess I should like start doing the crosswords.

WYMAN

They whittle away the hours.

JULIE

37 Across. "Strips in a chair." Five letters.

WYMAN

"Slats."

JULIE (smiling)

You mean, "sluts?"

WYMAN

That's "slattern." Eight letters. Doesn't fit. You must be thinking of lap dance.

JULIE

Yes. "Strips in a chair." What else could that mean?

WYMAN (raises glass)

Well, to words.

JULIE

How can you cheers alone?

WYMAN

Do you, want one? Help yourself.

JULIE

I like how you lick your teeth after the first taste.

(She then goes to refrigerator and takes a beer.)

Where's the opener?

WYMAN

It's twist off.

JULIE

Just kidding. I knew that.

WYMAN

It means co-responsible. Or almost co. Complicitous.

JULIE

Do you think I'm doing the right thing?

WYMAN

No.

JULIE

Throwing my life away? That's what Dad says. He was set on my becoming an actress really, or something special. Even teacher isn't good enough. The ugliest profession, he likes to joke, next to nurses. That gets my mom's goat.

WYMAN (laughing)

I might like him.

JULIE

My first role was the balloon girl in *Gypsy*. It was a nonspeaking part, but my dad was so stoked. But Mom said it was also for his own "aggrandizement." Her word.

WYMAN

You're sixteen. It's not like you have to decide now. About anything.

JULIE

I did a lot of political theater.

WYMAN

Musical theater?

JULIE

No. I went through a radicalized period when I was tween. Street theater. I was the youngest in the troop. Dad was not as proud. I don't see why not–it's not like I was a friggin' crack whore or something. Anyways, I always thought he secretly was sort of proud of me.

WYMAN

Very secretly! ...No, I'm sure he was. We live through our children, at a certain point. It's hard not to. No matter how well things went for you, in your own career, at a certain point the world begins to empty out. Which is why so many, at age forty, say, begin to go off the rails. ...Not to mention names.

JULIE

Did you, Wyman? (She drinks.) Sorry.

WYMAN

I did, yes, for a while. Around the age of forty.

JULIE

You were still in the Army?

WYMAN

Close to retirement.

JULIE

You did a makeover... like Madonna.

WYMAN

You mean, our Mother Mary?

JULIE

She did?

WYMAN

Just a joke. You don't get do-overs, I know that much.

JULIE

A fresh start?

WYMAN

I'll think about it. People don't change but maybe you can, once in a while, as you suggest, reinvent yourself. But what if you do it three or four times? What's the relation of number two to number four, for example? Or number three to number one? (He drinks.) Hand me the salt, will you?

JULIE

Now we're cooking with gas, as my father says. But we literally are, aren't we?

WYMAN

We are. You'll miss him, I can see.

JULIE

He'll chill, I hope.

WYMAN

And your mom?

JULIE

She married him at my age. So you see what a total hypocrite he is. Dad was fifteen years older. But Mom freaked, too: "You've got so much to do first," she said.

WYMAN

I think people spend their entire lives recreating the conditions of their childhood, no matter how good or bad it was. But that's another topic.

JULIE

But I'm still a child. You mean, my parents?

WYMAN

Todo. In the long run.

JULIE

Todo por amor?

(He looks at her, charmed.)

Maybe I'll study languages in college.

WYMAN

You're right, I suppose you're not recreating but creating. I don't know exactly when the recreating begins. Too soon. Some time right after the Garden of Eden, I suspect.

JULIE (softly)

Someday you'll tell me about your childhood?

WYMAN

A Midwestern one with an exotic mother. A New Yorker. Catholic. I guess we'll have time for that, if you're curious. My dad was a Protestant. A farm boy. He became a vet although he wanted to be a doctor.

JULIE

I'm sure I could learn a lot from you.

WYMAN

A crash course. Three months.

JULIE

But you'd be my father-in-law like forever.

WYMAN

Father-in-law? I must be getting old.

JULIE

Does it bother you?

WYMAN

Well, yeah, why wouldn't it? I'm starting to look like Mr. Potato Head.

JULIE

I played with him, too! You're my father's age. But you seem younger. He's way old school.

WYMAN

Doesn't sound like he wants to be a father-in-law, though. (He turns off the stove.) You're not just acting, I hope? I mean, for your sake. You're not, right?

JULIE

I totally think I would make good television.

WYMAN

What?

JULIE

You could see me on tv, couldn't you? I even know the sound track to my life.

> WYMAN

Ha. Of course. "When Johnny Comes Marching Home" is mine.

> JULIE

Not a Karaoke hit.

> WYMAN (charmed)

Wylie's got his hands full, I see.

> (As he goes for another beer, he sings a few bars of "When Johnny Comes Marching Home." As Wylie enters. Wylie looks at his dad and at Julie, who has a beer in her hand.)

> WYLIE (trying to keep positive)

Julie, you wouldn't believe my luck.

> JULIE

What?

> WYLIE

I qualify for a sign-up bonus.

> (Julie sets her beer down on the stove.)

> JULIE

Wow. Cool, Wylie. (To Wyman) Excuse us.

> (Julie and Wylie exit. Wyman wanders around the kitchen. Looks out the back window. Sits down at the table and drinks from his beer.)

Scene Six

Nighttime. Wyman and Wylie sit at the kitchen table. Wyman has a beer in front of him. Two sets of papers are before Wylie.

WYMAN

Is she asleep?

WYLIE

Yeah, just.

(Wyman sips his beer. Wylie shuffles through the papers.)

I need your signature on both.

WYMAN

They used to call it a "John Hancock."

WYLIE

I know. My declaration of independence.

WYMAN

Don't be so in a hurry. It's real out there. You should go to college. Out-of-state, if you want.

WYLIE

It's settled.

WYMAN

Not if I don't sign, it's not, is it?

WYLIE

I agreed to let her stay here, didn't I? And I won't tell her anything about your court...

WYMAN

I wasn't...you know that. It never came to that.

(Wyman gets up from the table.)

What the hell, a bribe and threat at once, by my own son. Not to mention keeping secrets from your own wife-to-be. What happened to you, Wylie? It was you who wanted her to stay her. I was just covering your ass after your impulsive, let's call it, decision to join the Army.

WYLIE (quietly)

Just sign, sir...please. Julie doesn't need to know all our baggage. It's way old, anyways. I only meant I know you could use the company. I don't like seeing you alone all the time. Of course in three months, I'll be back.

WYMAN

It's a four-year deal. She won't be able to go along all the time with you.

WYLIE

I know. Remember? I spent more than half my childhood without you around. This is important to me, Dad. I love her.

(Wyman sits.)

WYMAN

Since when? You guys barely know each other. You didn't think things through, Wylie.

(Wylie rises.)

WYLIE

Never mind then. I'll figure out some other shit, some other way.

WYMAN

How about a compromise?

WYLIE

What sort?

WYMAN

I sign one of them.

WYLIE (angry)

You'd let me get married to keep me out of the service? *That* is bribery. And then how would I support her? Just cause they fucked you, doesn't mean they'll fuck me! You fucked yourself!

>(Wyman rises as if to about to hit Wylie, but catches himself, and goes over to the refrigerator to get another beer. He sits back down.)

WYMAN

This whole conversation is ridiculous. You're seventeen, Wylie. I had such hopes for you.

WYLIE

And how old were you when you screwed up?

WYMAN

Look, things happen. If you've ever been in theater, you'd know. It was R&R. I regret it, but it's damn lonely at times.

WYLIE

Wow, the rules don't apply? How about all those times when Mom was lonely? And just me there to comfort her? When she cried herself to sleep at night.

WYMAN

Your mother? All she ever showed me was a stoic New Englander.

WYLIE

How wrong you are. And according to Mom, you had issues even before you joined.

WYMAN

I didn't even know your mom then. What crap.

WYLIE

She said it's why you joined. To hide.

WYMAN (angry)

Have it your way if it makes you feel better. One thing you might not realize is that it was because I was away—from you and your mother—that I did things I'm not so proud of. I would be sitting in Kuwait, in the damn desert, and be wondering what you and Mom were doing, and wondering how it was I wound up in Kuwait anyway. Stoicism doesn't meant you don't *have* emotions. And don't forget it happened *after* your mother left me. And took you with her. Anyway, Julie stays here, with me. She's too young to live out on her own.

WYLIE (loudly)

I already said...

WYMAN (quietly)

Okay, okay. Quiet. We don't want to wake her. (They listen together.) BT is hell—you'll barely have time to call her once a week. Where will they send you? Did they say?

WYLIE

They said Fort Knox.

WYMAN

Could be worse. Pretty country. Queer you chose Army. Did you know the Air Force should be part of the Army? Having a separate service like that is just a waste of money.

WYLIE

I would think you'd be pro defense.

WYMAN

I'm speaking as a taxpayer. (He grabs the pen from Wylie.) So which part of your life do you want me to sign away first?

WYLIE

What life? It doesn't matter which is first. Just sign, please.

WYMAN

Maybe it does, matter.

WYLIE

Like how could it?

WYMAN

If you're married, you might be able to get an age waiver. It might take months but...

WYLIE (almost pleading)

Why are you messing with me?

(Wyman rises.)

WYMAN

You've got to think through everything. All the possibilities. I told you, it's rough out there. One error of judgment can change everything. And Bush and the Republicans will never get over the fact that they no longer live in a gated community. It's all fear-mongering.

WYLIE

Are you going to sign or not, sir?

WYMAN

I'll sign. First, service.

(Wylie slides one set of papers over to Wyman.)

WYMAN

Those are the marriage papers.

WYLIE (coy)

Are they?

WYMAN

Do you know Othello?

WYLIE

I saw the movie.

WYMAN

It's not so much a flaw as a change of context that brought him down. He was good at war but tried to apply the same methods to love. You'll need clothes, toiletries, notepads, books, locks, etc. But skip the books. You won't have time to read. Anyway, it's time you moved on from *The Lord of the Rings*, wouldn't you say?

WYLIE

It's my life, isn't it?

(Wyman signs one set of papers and reaches over for the other set. He signs those as well.)

WYMAN

There, my John Hancock, twice.

Scene Seven

Two weeks later. Wylie has gone off to Basic Training. Wyman is in the livingroom watching TV when Julie comes into the room in her pajamas. She stands, moves around sheepishly, while he remains seated, his hand at the moment on the remote.

WYMAN

Why aren't you dressed? You haven't showered?

JULIE

Do I smell? A girl's got to smell good. (Looks toward the kitchen) I don't smell breakfast. When I was a girl scout I used to stay in the tent in my sleeping bag until I could smell breakfast. I never earned a single merit badge.

WYMAN

I'm serious. It's twenty till.

JULIE

It's dress down day at St. Anne's.

WYMAN

I'll dress you down unless you get ready.

JULIE

How long you been up?

WYMAN

Since five. Army habit. You made your bed?

(Julie sits on the arm of the couch.)

JULIE

Can...may I stay home today, Wyman?

WYMAN

You sick? Really?

JULIE

I have tummy ache.

WYMAN

Call your dad.

JULIE

You're my dad, too.

WYMAN

You're married, for Christ sakes. Call Wylie. I'm not going to the teacher-student conference either. (He turns back to TV, then back to her) Are you really sick? I've got Pepto-Bismol.

JULIE

When I was little I painted my walls a Pepto-Bismol pink. How about Pepsi?

WYMAN

We're out. You've been drinking those like...soda pop. When I was a kid my mom would give me Seven-Up. Said the carbonation was good for a stomach ache. Sometimes if it was really cold out–I mean, really cold, fifteen below, something you may never experience–she'd let me stay home from school. Sometimes she'd come into my room, which I shared with my younger brother–he slept with his eyes half-open–and I'd be playing possum and she'd let me sleep. Him too. My dad hated that. The farm animals didn't get a day off. When I was grown she told me how her own mother, back in Queens, would say to her sometimes: "Oh, why don't you stay home from school today?" "Oh, mama, I can't," she'd say. "Oh, just today, baby. Tomorrow you get there bright and early." It's funny to think of my mom as a young girl. My older brother never missed a day. He would study his pants off, go into his room–he had his own room–at night and just study. Or at least I think that's what he was doing.

JULIE

I would think he would be the favorite. She'd keep *him* home.

WYMAN

I see. "Ms. Psychiatrist."

JULIE

Just a psychologist. I haven't been to med-school yet.

WYMAN

So you know the difference?

JULIE

I do.

WYMAN

Oh, really. So which did you see?

JULIE

The latter. I wasn't that lame. I didn't need no doctor, just some counseling.

WYMAN

It's something I've always been interested in, psychology. I took a degree while in the Army–but in engineering, like most former farm boys. It wasn't Purdue, though. Speaking of Boilermakers, I think I'll...

JULIE (misses reference)

Why don't you go back to school, Wyman? And get off your ass!

(He laughs.)

WYMAN

Maybe. Who knows? But you won't get breakfast that way. Have you heard about getting more flies with honey? And it's you who should get to school.

JULIE

I might have the flu, be contagious. It doesn't have to be fifteen below to be cold. It's fifty-seven degrees out.

WYMAN

Fifty-seven...Impala.

JULIE

What?

WYMAN

It's not cold.

JULIE

Anyway, I don't like anyone to see me when I look gross.

WYMAN

You don't look gross. Just shower.

JULIE

Feel gross, then.

WYMAN

What would we do here? Fly a kite?

JULIE

Watch *Titanic*. Make popcorn. Cuddle on the couch—whoops. My bad. (She laughs.) Laugh ourselves silly. I could give you a haircut. You can drink.

WYMAN

I do that anyway.

JULIE

How about not drink then?

WYMAN

Oh, so you're trying to change me already. Thanks for waiting two weeks.

> (He drops the remote, goes to the kitchen, takes out a beer from the refrigerator, and opens it. She sits down on the couch and changes the channel. He returns beer in hand.)

Breakfast.

JULIE

Alrighty then. Maybe not not drink.

WYMAN

I was watching that you know. And that's my seat.

> JULIE (scooting over and holding out the remote)

The cooking channel?

WYMAN

It's not too early for you to learn, as you're married.

> (He takes the remote from her and sits down next to her on the couch. He sets the remote aside without changing the channel.)

JULIE

Are you like addicted?

WYMAN (holding up beer)

You mean this? I crossed over to the other side some time ago.

JULIE

Is it exotic there?

WYMAN

No.

JULIE

Well, what does it look like there? Describe it.

WYMAN

I see everyone at right angles.

JULIE

Including me?

WYMAN

Not you. That's what's surprising. But Wylie, yes. His mother, for sure.

(She waits.)

I'll use an analogy. There's a ghost town in Arizona called Jerome. It's high on the hill. Alone up there. A mile up. Of course it's a tourist trap now. But still you get the sense of what happens when everyone leaves. When the money runs out. And the jobs. And all you've got are buildings. The old bank. The jail. The small shops. Everything like at right angles to the other. But not exactly right angles either. Time has taken a toll. The buildings lean a bit. Separate. The jail in fact has slid half way down a slope. And all the while no people.

JULIE

Spooky.

(He raises his beer.)

WYMAN

Breakfast?

JULIE

Okay.

WYMAN

No tummy ache?

JULIE

I'm thinking about Chernobyl. People worse off than I am. Not funny, I guess.
Did you see war?

WYMAN

Yes.

JULIE

Kill anyone?

WYMAN

From a distance.

JULIE

What was it like? The service. Dramatic?

WYMAN

You mean, like describe it?

(She smiles, and waits.)

WYMAN

Everything is directed toward a single purpose and each person has an assigned status and role. And a strict, quasi-religious code of conduct. To not lie, for starters. Or, for example, should you be found consorting with another soldier's wife, you could be subject to three years in the brig. For "simple" adultery. (He rises from the couch and stand looking out at the audience, his back to her.) And of course, once you begin it's near impossible to cut things off. That's why it's best never to begin. You never know what you'll get a taste for. (Turns to her) You get my meaning? But I was good at Army. I'm a morning person. And a military man needs some kid in him.

(He remains standing.)

JULIE

When I was twelve, I used to get up for early Mass because I was hot for an altar boy. My mom thought I'd become suddenly religious.

WYMAN

Are you?

JULIE

I like the sound of Latin.

WYMAN

And what happened with the altar boy?

JULIE

Nothing. The priest caught on—and made me pay. Father Donahue.

WYMAN

He didn't...

JULIE

Get up in my business? No. He made me confess. Made me come to confession every morning and confess totally everything.

WYMAN

That bugger. Or maybe that's the wrong word.

JULIE

My dad used to say I was a real bugger.

WYMAN (laughing)

Usually that's used for boys.

JULIE (not getting it)

Was Wylie?

WYMAN

Wylie was off in his room much of the time. He got used to my being deployed, I guess. Had to learn to entertain himself. Especially as he was an only child. He liked D&D a lot.

JULIE

Dungeons and Dragons?

WYMAN

Yeah. So much for baseball cards.

(They look at each other, not speaking.)

WYMAN

Okay, just this once—get the movie. But you've seen it a million times, I expect. I'll make some popcorn.

JULIE

Should I shower?

WYMAN

I think I can stand it.

> (He exits and she goes to her room to get
> the movie. She returns and pops the video
> in the DVD. He returns with the popcorn
> and sits down next to her.)

The beauty of microwave.

JULIE

I mean, seriously, maybe you should go back to school, Wyman?

WYMAN

Hey, man, get off my ass. Or hymen get off my ass. Whatever.

JULIE

That was random. But it's cool you said "whatever."

WYMAN

Yeah, I'm a hepcat. Maybe I should just go back to high school instead.

JULIE

No, you need a master's, young man. My dad says everyone needs one these days. It's his big regret. (She tries the popcorn.) You could do it, for me.

WYMAN

For you?

JULIE

Make me proud. (More popcorn) The Superhero never gives up.

WYMAN

Whatever. Just turn that light out, will you.

(As she reaches toward the lamp, her breasts
are exposed. She turns out the light. We see
her pick up the remote and start the movie.)

WYMAN

For your information, young lady, I've already enrolled. I started yesterday.

(The movie appears on the butterfly screen.)

JULIE

Wow. Where? And you didn't say anything?

WYMAN

I have my secrets. At UCLA.

JULIE

Wow. They let you in? Awesome. That's where I want to go.

(She turns to him and quickly kisses him on
the lips. Startled, he draws back.)

WYMAN

Whoa. For?

JULIE

Exceeding expectations.

WYMAN

Where did you learn that phrase?

JULIE (archly)

Teachers use it. I'm going to be a teacher, you know.

WYMAN

Oh, really. Well, take this, smarty pants.

>(He tickles her. They wrestle on the couch, Wyman knocking over his beer in the process onto the floor. He starts to reach for it.)

JULIE

Leave it.

>(She grabs the remote and pauses the movie, and is on top of him. She goes for his belt buckle.)

BLACKOUT

END OF ACT ONE

Act Two

Scene Eight

Between scenes we hear a non-vocal version of "Johnny Comes Marching Home" in the background. It's two weeks later. Wyman is wearing jeans, a white t-shirt, and flip-flops. The door to Wylie's bedroom is closed. Wyman knocks, and then cracks open the door.

WYMAN

Breakfast.

(He closes the door. We see him in the kitchen setting two places. He goes to the refrigerator and takes out orange juice. He pours two glasses, and then adds a little vodka to his.)

(Calling to the bedroom)

Breakfast.

(He sits at the table and reads through the paper. He starts to do a crossword puzzle. He sips his drink. He gets up and goes to the stove. Julie enters in her Catholic school girl uniform but is still barefoot, shoes and socks in hand. She leans against the counter top.)

JULIE (forced cheerfulness)

Pretty fast, huh? Someday you'll let me see you in uniform.

(awkward silence)

WYMAN

Maybe.

(He rises, goes over to the stove.)

Do they rap your knuckles if you come late?

JULIE

It's not like back-in-the-day, I told you.

WYMAN

No, I suppose nothing is.

(Silence. Julie and Wyman look at each other.)

JULIE

I'm surprised he got early leave. The month went fast. Not that I've seen you much the last two weeks.

WYMAN (ignoring last comment)

Hope it's not a bad sign, a leave during Basic Training. Seems irregular. But for you and me, it's best, no doubt. He's due at eight tonight.

JULIE

I know. (She takes her orange juice off the table) Are you worried?

WYMAN

It was his idea leaving you here.

JULIE (mildly sarcastic)

Oh really? And to use his college fund, for St. Anne's?

WYMAN

That too. He knows about it. We don't want any high school dropouts in the family.

JULIE

Hey!

(She again leans against the counter.)

I barely remember him. Isn't that insane?

WYMAN

What's the webcam for then?

JULIE

That's only once a week.

WYMAN

It's only been four weeks.

JULIE

He seems changed, Wyman. I shouldn't say that I'm sure. As he's your son.

WYMAN

What do you mean changed? Maybe he hears something in your voice. Wylie's sharp. As a kid, he was a wiz. What did he say? He hasn't called *me* once.

JULIE

He says the Army's a test—that it's what he wanted. A challenge. For both of us, he said—which was sort of weird. He says he so misses me. But does he know me? God, if he knew.

WYMAN

Anyway, you're his wife now. Think of it as an arranged marriage.

JULIE

My parents never speaking to me again. Funny sort of arranged marriage.

> (Wyman turns the bacon in the pan, his back to her. Julie hops up on the kitchen counter. She begins putting on her socks and shoes. We see her panties.)

WYMAN

I'm going away so you guys will have some privacy.

JULIE

What? Where? You don't have to. Don't be retarded.

> (Wyman turns to look at her. He notices her panties. Turns back to the pan.)

WYMAN (determinedly offhand)

The Philippines. Just for a week. I mean, after he arrives. It's Spring break for me, too. Sort of.

JULIE

It would be weird without you here. We've never been entirely alone, Wylie and I.

WYMAN (glancing at her sideways)

That's the idea. It's called marriage. You're waiting at home for the return of your warrior. (She looks at him.) I'm serious. I'm more traditional than you might think, about some things. (She remains silent.) And I said *some* things.

JULIE (pleading)
Please? You won't be in the way, Wyman. Not at all.

WYMAN (he turns more directly)
I need a Spring Break. And I like the Philippines, Asia's laggard or not.

JULIE

Traitor.

> (Seeing he is uncomfortable, she balls up her arms around her knees. Tries to change the subject.)

So how do they treat you? You have a clique?

WYMAN

Eh?

JULIE
I mean at the school. You've been like gone these two weeks.

WYMAN
I think you know why. As for at school, I'm a curiosity. Becoming a psychologist at my age? Must be a loser. I tell them my professional interest in adolescent sexuality is a product of growing up in the 60's. There were no teenagers prior to 1950, I tell them. Did you know, the word wasn't even invented until 1941? You need a car of your own, and a few greenbacks in your pocket, to be a teenager. That will be my thesis! Which I was born without!

> (Julie doesn't get it.)

Thesis envy.

JULIE

You mean...I get it.

(Now fully dressed, she hops down and sits
at the table.)

So I'm like subject matter. It's mind-bottling.

WYMAN

Boggling.

JULIE

I knew that.

WYMAN

No, not just subject matter. But you asked.

JULIE

Did you have a car back then?

WYMAN

No. No money either. But I had...an imagination. Uncle Sam works that way.
Promising adventure.

JULIE

Seriously, if you go, you'll only see him for like one day. He joined because of
you, you know. Wants you to be proud of him. You've got the Gulf War over
him.

WYMAN

Did he say that?

JULIE

No, not exactly that.

WYMAN

I didn't think so. He joined so he could support you, remember? In the manner to which you've become accustomed, as my wife had it. And she had.

JULIE

Which is what?

WYMAN

Well, you have your own room.

JULIE

I heard you again last night.

WYMAN

I'm rehearsing for a play.

(Julie laughs, but then is more serious)

JULIE

You know what I mean...the nightmares. What's up with that? You woke me up. It sounded like Macbeth if it was a play.

WYMAN (dissembling further)

Sorry. Blame the Sisters. Catholic school was rough back then. In fifth grade I was paddled for cutting up.

JULIE

Did it hurt?

WYMAN

Damn straight. The kids in the room, including my girlfriend, Jill, could hear me cry out on each swat, as the sound of the swat and then my yell echoed down the corridor.

JULIE

They can't do that now.

WYMAN

(laughing) You mean "Corporal" punishment? "General," either, for that matter.

JULIE

I don't buy it. Not as far as the nightmares go. I'll get it out of you somehow.

(She realizes what she has said.)

I mean...

WYMAN

Every word is fraught now. Like we're overhearing ourselves.

JULIE

May I ask you something?

WYMAN

No, I don't have a tattoo.

JULIE

I know, remember?

WYMAN (a bit distracted)

But I'm a marked man, ha. (He turns off the stove.) Anyway, you kids don't count that, isn't that right? And it doesn't count if it was only once? Or so I've been trying to tell myself these last two weeks. But you had a question?

JULIE

It's taken me two weeks to–but did it mean something to you? Even though it was just, you know, as you said. I mean, did it count?

WYMAN

Yes, of course. But it can't, can it? And for you?

JULIE

More than I wanted it to.

WYMAN

Even though it was just...and I did all the taking? And Leonardo Dicaprio did all the talking, though I can't say I remember what he was saying at that moment.

JULIE

I'm being serious, Wyman.

WYMAN

I know. That's what worries me. If it meant something, it can't.

JULIE

It did anyway. And it meant more that it wasn't selfish. I wanted you to be happy.

WYMAN

Then I guessed we're fucked. (Laughs ruefully) Because we can't do anything about it–nothing further. You know that, don't you? I'm not up for Greek tragedy.

JULIE

Oedipus Rex? We read that.

WYMAN

Electra. Father-daughter. But that's one thing I don't get. You have a father.

JULIE

He loves me, but he's distant. Ever since I turned twelve. He can't really show it–da love. Anyway, Wylie won't know. How could he? You don't have to go.

WYMAN

Maybe he won't. I don't know. I don't want to think about it, really. Let's talk about something else, okay? It excites me just to talk about it.

(We sense he wants to go to Julie, hold her.)

JULIE

It does? Why do people feel bad about desires? Sex?

(He places eggs and bacon on two plates and sets the plates on the table.)

WYMAN

Eat it before it gets cold.

(He sits.)

It's funny though–we feel guilty about wanting to fuck our own wife. Perhaps the ownership part of it feels wrong. I mean, once you're married you're co-owners. And you can't lend your body out to others!

JULIE

Like I did.

WYMAN

Well, I'm not blaming you...anyway, it wasn't your whole body.... I mean I think Freud was trying to answer that question: Why do we feel bad? I mean, I don't feel bad about wanting to play golf, usually. His answer: mum and dad. "Our beds are crowded," he said.

JULIE

Did you love her? Wylie's mom.

WYMAN

One time, in the middle of sex, she said: "There's something wrong with you." It was the beginning of the end, I think, looking back. Things are ending before we realize that's what's happening. Same for beginnings. Anyway, women don't look back–they've already done their mourning. (He drinks, sets his glass down.) Sorry for the philosophy. No more questions, okay?

(She switches the two glasses, sips his.)

JULIE

You're starting early.

WYMAN

I am.

(Again, we see he wants to touch her.)

Shouldn't you be getting to school?

(She shifts in her chair.)

JULIE

I could stay home.

(He leans back. Then leans forward, a bit menacingly, his eyes on her.)

WYMAN

A four-letter word?

JULIE (into the game)

You mean "home"?

WYMAN

I might mean "mean."

JULIE (excited)

Are you? Have you been?

WYMAN

Have you heard of "PTSD"?

JULIE

It's a kind of "STD"?

WYMAN (laughing)

You could say that.

JULIE

But you can't, say it? Anyway, I don't believe it, that you're mean.

WYMAN

But what if it's not me, young lady? What if it's someone else?

(Wyman get up from the table, gets another beer from the fridge, and stands next to her as if asking for, or demanding oral sex)

JULIE (looking up at him, a little fearful now)

I will if you want.

(Wyman waits. She starts to unbucle his belt. He, as if coming to, moves away, turns his back to her. Buckles his belt.)

WYMAN

Sorry. Don't want to add daymares. … Or any mares.

(Julie, regaining her composure, rises and takes her plate to the sink, starts to rinse it.)

Leave it, you'll be late for school.

JULIE

Thanks. Not quite so brutal a regimen around here as Wylie led me to believe.

WYMAN (again on notice)

Led you to believe? (Then again more calmly) Yeah, I'm getting soft in my old age, I guess. Softening of the brain, I think they used to call it.

(She grabs her backpack. Starts toward the back door, then turns back to him.)

JULIE

Still hope you don't go to the Philippines.

(She exits. Wyman sits.)

WYMAN

"Brutal?"

Scene Nine

That evening. Wylie's room. His sword still hangs above the bed. His Army backpack and duffle bag rest in a corner. Julie is under the covers. Wylie is undressing, his back to us. His hair is cut short, Army style. When he removes his shirt, we see a large shield tattoo on his back. He stands by the bed in his underwear.

WYLIE

What's this about my dad going out of town tomorrow night? The Philippines?

JULIE

He said we needed a honeymoon.

WYLIE

Do you? We could go someplace.

JULIE

I thought you'd like some home cooking. (She sits up, shyly holding the sheet to her breasts.) We can play house.

WYLIE

We're married.

JULIE (taken aback)

Is that how married people talk?

WYLIE

Sorry. It's just that I feel like he's avoiding me. I'm sure he's disappointed in me. But I can do college later, right? (He smiles.) I have a surprise for you.

> (He turns his back to her. She gasps when she sees his tattoo.)

I think of it as a symbol of our marriage. Now—before was child's play.

JULIE (still unsure.)

It's...tight. You're my Achilles...

WYLIE

Heal?

JULIE

You mean, "hile"? (Sheepishly) Sorry.

WYLIE (mildly)

I see you've been infected by Dad's wordplay.

JULIE

Swordplay. Oops. (Half to herself) Funny sleeping under your sword.

WYLIE

I missed this room. But funny, base feels like home, too. Even the hut.

JULIE

What hut?

WYLIE

SWA hut. Like they use in Southwest Asia. Twenty to a room. All wood, except the roof is metal, which of course amplifies the rain and it sure rains a lot in Kentucky. Makes the grass blue, I guess.

JULIE

You've put some muscle on. Does the Army allow tattoos?

WYLIE

Long as it doesn't show in uniform. They're pretty desperate for recruits. Some of the guys in Basic are pretty poor readers. What's got into my dad? School? He's forty-five. Did you have something to do with this?

JULIE

Your dad's a smart man. He says he saw all kinds in the service, perfect for a psychologist. He's...

WYLIE (not listening)

I couldn't see an alternative. I mean, it all happened so fast. You don't regret it, no wedding ceremony–just Dad as witness–do you?

JULIE

Oh just come to bed, Wylie. I want to touch it. You're like a man now. Complete.

(He hesitates.)

WYLIE

No, tell me: was it weird? Did he try anything? He gets drunk, I know. And there are other things.

JULIE (curious)

Are there?

WYLIE

Yes. Why do you want to know so bad? You think he's some sort of puzzle?

JULIE

Dude, you brought him up. I didn't say anything about some sort of fascination. I don't know why you're super cross.

WYLIE

I don't want to always be talking about him, understand. He has a way of always being the center of attention. It was always about his career. Well, I'm not a kid anymore. I'm a married man. I've got my own life to live.

JULIE (dropping the sheet)

Okay—what do I have to say? Come on then. He's in the other room. I just heard him. Come to bed, Wylie. Hurry. I'm excited.

WYLIE (half-joking)

I can see that. (He takes off his pants.) You didn't get the scissors, did you?

> (Wylie climbs in bed. Julie moaning. The butterfly screen lights up.)

Scene Ten

Morning. The three of them sit at the kitchen table. A box of Wheaties is on the table. The men are dressed for the day, but Julie is in pj's and is barefoot.

WYMAN (to Wylie)

Beer?

WYLIE

Sir? This is a first.

WYMAN

Well, it's Spring Break. I leave at five. (Pointing to the beer) Julie?

JULIE

Sure.

> (Wyman gets up, goes to the refrigerator, and, returning, sets a twelve pack on the table.)

WYLIE

Isn't she underage?

> WYMAN

You, too, technically. Don't quibble.

> WYLIE

(skeptical) So you two have been having Octoberfest while I was away?

> JULIE

Not even. It's just a beer.

> WYLIE

I didn't know you *liked* beer. Most girls your age like....*Sex on the Beach*.

> JULIE (half-joking)

My parents gave me permission to marry, didn't they. In the end, anyway. I guess I'm old enough to drink a beer.

> WYMAN

I never understood that either.

> WYLIE (eyeing the two of them)

Either?

> JULIE (ignoring Wylie)

I told you, Wyman, remember? I was ruined. So it totally didn't matter after that. After sex, you're supposed to marry. Old school Catholicism. I'm their only child.... Like Wylie is...yours. I hadn't really thought of that before. Two only children.

> WYMAN

That's what I mean, an only child. And disown you, to boot. Not right in my book.

> WYLIE (on another tack)

When did you tell him all this I'd like to know?

JULIE

I've lived here almost two months.

WYLIE (skeptical)

Fine.

WYMAN (half to himself)

Still, I still don't get it. This is 2001. People don't marry because they lose their virginity.

WYLIE

Can we talk about something else?

WYMAN

Sure.

(Wyman stands, walks away from the table.)

Are they treating you okay?

WYLIE

It's the Army, Dad.

WYMAN

Do you like it?

WYLIE

Yes, sir, I do.

WYMAN

It's okay if you don't have other options. Not that I'm not proud of you. Just don't make a career of it.

WYLIE

You did. Until...

WYMAN (abruptly)

At least there's no war.

WYLIE (bitterly)

No competition for you, eh?

WYMAN

What's that supposed to mean?

JULIE

Boys, please. We only have today together. I wish you wouldn't go, Wyman? It makes me feel... like responsible.

WYLIE (softening)

You can stay, Dad.

WYMAN

I've got a ticket. Nonrefundable. And for your information, Wylie, one mistake does not....

> (Wyman goes back to the table, picks up and cracks another beer, and walks away from the table again.)

Forget it.

JULIE (curious)

What, Wyman?

WYMAN

Nothing.

WYLIE (to Wyman)

Are you okay?

WYMAN

Don't patronize me. I've been to hell and back.

WYLIE (regretting solicitousness)

When does the statute of limitations run out? You've got to move on.

WYMAN

You're telling me?

JULIE

Is that what those nightmares were?

WYLIE (to Julie)

How would you know about his nightmares?

JULIE (covering up)

What did I just say to you? I've been living here.

> (Wylie, unconvinced, rises from the ta-
> ble and looks at his dad and then at Julie.
> Downs his beer.)

WYLIE (half to himself)

What the hell went down here? (Then) Julie?

JULIE

What do you mean, what the hell?

WYLIE

What do you think I mean?

JULIE (voice breaking, but accusatory)

You wanted me staying here, right?

WYLIE

Where else would you have stayed? I didn't know your parents would dis you, did I? It wasn't like I liked leaving you here. With him.

JULIE

You wanted someone to look after him, too, right?

WYLIE

What gave you that idea?

JULIE

It's part of the idea I got out of it.

WYLIE

What are you saying? I'm not stupid, you know.

JULIE

You could have taken me with you. Why didn't you? Why?

WYLIE

I told you, it's not allowed during Basic. Not on base.

WYMAN

Who's on first?

JULIE

Wyman!

WYMAN

Sorry. That was childish. But I don't like you two implying that I need looking after. It's not like I haven't made my own way in the world. Ever since I was eighteen. Anyway, what's done is done. So let's be cool about it. Cool it. Wylie.

WYLIE (to Julie)

Done? (to Julie) Tell me what happened here. Julie? You're my wife. I thought about you the whole time I was gone.

(She lays her head down on the table.)

WYMAN

Give her a break, Wylie. She was just concerned about me. My nightmares have been worse since you left. It brought back a lot of the feelings I had about leaving you and your mother for the war. And other times.

WYLIE

Don't give me that, Dad. I know what your nightmares are about.

WYMAN

Is that right.

(She raises her head, looks at Wyman, and then Wylie.)

JULIE

I'm not sure I'm getting all this. Just answer me straight, Wylie. Why did you leave me here?

WYLIE

How many times do I have to say it?

(She waits.)

WYLIE

He wouldn't sign the permit otherwise.

JULIE

Marriage?

WYLIE

Both. I needed parental permission for the Army, too. Ask him.

JULIE

Wyman?

WYMAN

That's not a hundred percent accurate. I made no requests. But yes, I had to sign. For both. Surely you knew about the marriage permit, Julie.

JULIE

I didn't think about it. Wylie said nothing. You could have told me, Wylie. We were getting married. (to Wyman) Why did *you* want me here?

WYMAN

I didn't think off-base was a good place for you. You're way too young. You've got school. And Wylie seemed to want it. (to Wylie) Didn't you?

JULIE (to Wyman)

So you did it for him?

WYLIE

More like *to* me.

JULIE

I still don't get it.

WYMAN

Well, I told you, remember?

WYLIE (mocking)

Yeah, remember?

JULIE

Told me what?

WYMAN (ignoring Wylie)

I grew up in the 60's, the transition. I've never gotten over it. (Sips his beer) I remember a spread in *Look* magazine. About teens experimenting. I was like maybe ten. It was pretty radical. Especially for a kid from Indiana. But now it's even more powerful. It's like a foreign country. You are, embarrassing as it is to say it. In front of Wylie. (Turning to Wylie) Though he knows the most of it. In fact, he's egging me on just now, so I will say it. It's more important to him, apparently, than anything between you two. (Back to Julie) For all I know, he wanted to see this come to pass.

WYLIE (standing up)

Jesus, that takes the cake. I've totally had it.

WYMAN

And can eat it, too.

WYLIE

And wash it down with beer, sir?

WYMAN

Whatever. So maybe I've become a drunk. I'm entitled. You never saw what I saw, did you? At least haven't yet. Or have had your wife walk out on you... (Stops, realizing he doesn't want to go there) But for your sake, Wylie, I'll say it. I was discharged early, Julie. So now, you know. It's in the open.

JULIE (anger yet intimacy)

You mean you kept me here on purpose? O my god, Wyman.

WYMAN

It wasn't so clear cut as that, as you recall. So let's be accurate. You didn't object, did you?

JULIE

You sounded like Wylie just then.

WYLIE

And that's so bad, Julie?

JULIE

I didn't mean it that way...

WYLIE (overlapping)

Not that I care now anyway.

JULIE

I meant, hating on me.

WYLIE

I'm getting it—that's why you wanted to come to my house in the first place.

JULIE

You forget I didn't know your mother was gone.

WYMAN (half to himself)

You needed a place to stay. I knew better. I thought I'd be okay. A test, of sorts. I'm sorry. I am.

JULIE

What do you mean "early"? For what exactly? A girl? Please, Wyman?

WYLIE

Tell her, sir. I want to watch—isn't that what *you* are accusing *me* of? Some sort of bogus psychological inversion. So, cool, I'm watching. She's referring to "discharged early." Well?

WYMAN

I don't think this is the time.

WYLIE

When would be appropriate exactly?

WYMAN

Okay, Private, I will tell her. But for her sake. Since you, like a woman Wylie, won't take any responsibility for this. (to Julie) The timing worked out, shall we say. I was a month shy of my twenty. The Army didn't want a scandal. I was a decorated officer. It was a girl, yes. She was sixteen.

> (Julie gets up from the table and stands framed by the back door. Wyman sits. Wylie has moved toward the bedroom door.)

JULIE

Sixteen, Wyman?

WYLIE

I knew it. God. (to Wyman) I could turn you in. She's underage on top of everything else.

> (Wyman hides his head in his hands.)

JULIE (to Wylie)

And you? Dude, you knew all this? You were testing me? (She thinks.) Testing him? This was some sort of creeper experiment?

WYLIE

Of course not. You're turning this on me? You're the slut, Julie, right?

WYMAN (standing)

Hey! That's enough.

JULIE (to herself)

Or maybe, man, maybe it was you, Wylie, who wanted me because I was sixteen. For him!

WYLIE (ignoring her)

Enough, is it? I don't fucking think so.

> (Wylie calmly walks into his bedroom and returns with his sword. He holds it front of him with two hands, points it at his dad.)

Remember when Mom found out?

JULIE (jerked back to present)

Wylie!

> (Wylie raises it above his head as if to bring it down upon his dad's head. The butterfly screen flickers. Wyman doesn't flinch or bow his head.)

Wyman!

> (Frustrated, Wylie slashes the twelve-pack
> of beer, and then tosses the sword on the
> floor.)

WYLIE

I'm fucking out of here. But be sure he includes all the details, Julie. The girl was banished from her family. A Kuwaitee. She's lucky she wasn't stoned to death. Her only choice was exile. At least I've got the Army, huh, Dad? Maybe I'll find a war. Enjoy yourself, Julie. You two deserve...

WYMAN

Enough, Wylie... please. You're talking to your wife.

WYLIE

Ex. I'm talking to my ex-wife. My wife of two months. Isn't that a joke. Your one-month lover–better yet. Why don't you take her to the Philippines with you?

> (Wyman and Julie look at each other.)

WYMAN

It isn't as you imagine it to be. It was only, oral...once.

WYLIE

"Oral." Perfect for a wordsmith.

> (Wylie goes into his bedroom. Julie moves
> to pick up the pieces of glass.)

WYMAN

Leave it until later. You don't have any shoes on.

> (But Julie kneels and, head bowed, starts to
> pick up shards)

WYMAN

I'll call your dad.

JULIE (raising her head, pleading)

No. Isn't there another way?

WYMAN (stoically)

My flight's in seven hours. I'll see you on the other side of Spring Break.

> (She doesn't answer, and is still kneeling when Wylie reappears, holding his backpack and duffle bag.)

WYLIE

I'm going to my mom's. Something I should have done a long time ago. And I'm taking the car.

> (Wylie exits through kitchen door.)

WYMAN (calling after him)

Wylie, you're in no shape to drive right now. Wylie...

> (Again, "Johnny Comes Marching Home," but this time a vocal rendition)

Scene Eleven

A tattoo parlor, summer. Wyman and Julie sit in chairs waiting her turn. Julie is in tank top and shorts.

WYMAN

I don't approve of this. One tattoo is enough for anybody.

JULIE

Seriously, you don't have to stay, Wyman.

WYMAN

In for a penny, in for a pound...of flesh.

(Julie laughs.)

JULIE

So how was the Philippines?

WYMAN

Familiar. Like Mexico. But they seem to wear the colonial history more easily. And MacArthur, after all, is their hero.

JULIE

MacArthur?

WYMAN

Sometimes I forget how young you are.

JULIE

Do you? (Gesturing with a mocking two finger call-me sign) Why didn't you call? It's been two months.

WYMAN

I checked in with your father.

JULIE

You did? He didn't say. He doesn't know anything.

WYMAN

Well, I don't imagine he would have spoken to me had he.

JULIE

Are you still a student?

WYMAN

No.

JULIE

It's not on me?

WYMAN

No. I think I'll travel more. Maybe Cambodia next. I study the culture through its cuisine. It's food. Very pleasant. But no more nonrefundable tickets. You're studying hard, I trust.

JULIE

Yes, still want to be that teacher.

WYMAN

I think they only allow one tattoo at St. Anne's. Not to mention what your parents will say. Witnessing this seems like a further betrayal on my part.

JULIE

I didn't know who else to ask. No one will know about the tattoo right off— (laughing) this one is not on the ankle.

WYMAN

I'm afraid to ask. Is it a snowflake?

JULIE

No, but it flies.

WYMAN

A fly?

(Julie laughs. Wyman picks up a magazine, opens it, and then closes it again.)

WYMAN

No new love life?

JULIE

No. Why? Would that excite you? (Whispering voice) Was that part of it with Wylie?

WYMAN

Desire may be triangular. Love not.

JULIE (hopeful)

Love?

WYMAN

Some people's lives just shouldn't be a part of other people's lives.

JULIE

Why?

WYMAN

You know perfectly well. It's...it's not done. (Sort of bemused) Or at least hasn't been recently.

JULIE

I'm even legal in some states. Anyway, I won't always be seventeen.

WYMAN

Seventeen? My god, when was your birthday? I'm sorry.

JULIE

That's okay. My family made a big deal about it. I'm using my birthday money for this! They'd kill me. But it's not like it's crack.

WYMAN (serious)

You know, if you ever need anything you can call me.

JULIE

I did. I think I'm up next. I'll show you what it is when it's done.

WYMAN

Not sure that's a good idea.

JULIE

I get you. Aren't men sad?

(Wyman again fidgets with a magazine.)

WYMAN

Well, I'd be *happy* to keep up the tuition, if your parents can't. It would make me happy to.

JULIE (gently)

Guilt?

WYMAN (smiling)

Maybe a little.

JULIE

They can afford St. Anne's. But I think they think it's like no longer appropriate for me...although the Church gave me an annulment. For a price. I want to go to public school anyways. Wear my own clothes. Save the money for Wylie. I'm sure the G.I. Bill won't cover totally everything.

(A moment of silence.)

When does he deploy?

WYMAN

I don't know exactly. He won't speak to me. But soon he'll get his orders, according to his mother. I spoke with her the other day. First time in years. It would be our eighteenth anniversary next month.

JULIE

Was Wylie an accident?

WYMAN

We were planning to marry anyway. He's learning Arabic, I understand.

JULIE

I'll be praying for him.

(She stands up. As she heads to the tattoo chair, she gently touches Wyman's arm.)

WYMAN

Will it hurt?

JULIE (turning back to look at him)

Yes.

(She sits in a reclining chair. The black light comes back on. Butterflies that turn into flying scissors fill the space.)

END OF PLAY

School Play

A Play in Two Acts

Characters

Ted, forty-five, white, part-time college English instructor
Charles, twenty, black Kenyan, college student
George, sixty, white, administrator, former military
Ji, fifteen, Korean high school student
Yi, thirty-five, Ji's mother
Hung, ten, Ji's brother
Lya, fifteen, Korean, Ji's high school friend
Dick, twenty-five, white, muscular, high school maintenance man
College Student 1, male
College Student 2, female
Principal Samuels, black male
Two other college students
George's "secretary," a young woman (nonspeaking)
Two policemen (nonspeaking)

The action takes place at an urban high school in Los Angeles.

Act One

October. A phone conversation. Ted is standing outside the wrought-iron gates of Cleveland High School. His leather briefcase rests on a stone bench. Ted is handsome, thin, sallow. Brilliant and shipwrecked. There is a tree to one side. George stands in a back spotlight, next to a desk. He is a big, gregarious fellow. But he is no fool. Both men speak into cell phones.

TED

The only real question I had was whether there is security at the high school after school lets out.

GEORGE

No, there isn't, Ted. No budget for that. But we've never had a problem at our off-site campuses. Not a peep. I know it's easy to feel isolated at that hour of the day. I don't mean to say I'm not hearing you.

TED

It's dark when we finish. I mean black. Like the cover to a bible.

GEORGE (chuckling)

That's why we don't offer night classes at high schools anymore. Just afternoon classes. But we've passed the darkest day of the year. You finish at six, right? Be light at eighteen hours pretty soon, my boy.

TED

I suppose, yes.

GEORGE

I'd be happy to talk to the young man. I was Army before becoming a principal and I was a high school principal before assuming my present position at the college. I know it can get hairy, I've...

TED (impatient)

No need. I can talk to him if need be—I've been teaching a long time. Part-time mostly. Never a college class at a high school campus however. I've done practically everything else though. Even prison. That classroom reeked of cigarettes. (Musing) Smoking almost their only outlet. (Back to the present) No, my only real question is whether there is security. Someone on duty. Someone responsible.

GEORGE

I'm afraid not. Only a janitor. Until five. But I want you to know, Ted, that you have institutional support. Don't hesitate to call me—you have my direct line now.

> (A young woman, perhaps George's secretary, appears at the edge of his spotlight. He raises his index finger to indicate, "One minute.")

TED

So you'll know, we were kicked out of one classroom. Now we're in F-1.

> (The woman leaves George's office.)

GEORGE

I'll write that down.

> (He doesn't.)

(Rhetorically) Teachers are territorial, aren't they?

TED

A drama teacher. Said he would be having rehearsals in the classroom after school. Said they would be doing *The Importance of Being Earnest*. Haven't seen hide nor hair of him since. Leaves right when the bell rings, right at three p.m., I suspect.

GEORGE

Well, I'd be happy to bring both matters up with the principal at Cleveland. He's a good guy–Willie Samuels. Runs a good school. He's been there quite a while. A black fellow. Deaf in one ear. An old football injury, I think. He's nearing retirement.

TED

Well I haven't even come across him. What time does *he* leave campus?

GEORGE

Around four, I think.

TED

My student is from Africa.

GEORGE

Is he? What's his name?

TED

Charles.

GEORGE

Black?

TED

Yeah. It's just I'm thinking he may have seen a lot. In Africa. I put on his essay, "Don't be a fool," when he mentioned wanting to buy an AK-47. He mentioned, too, that he'd started drinking beer recently and found he couldn't stop sometimes. And when he started drinking he thought about things, about what he could do with a girl for one thing, for example, but that he'd lost his girlfriend. His father kicked him out of the house right after high school. He lives with his uncle, he wrote...has a room there. At his uncle's house.

GEORGE

Well, as I was saying...

TED

Oh, I'm sure things will be fine. You know how sometimes your imagination gets the best of you. He is an intelligent boy. Very handsome. Writes well, lots of promise. Blackest person I ever saw. Another shade of black. He hasn't done anything threatening in class really. He's just, as I said, quietly quarrelsome. Corrects other students. Sometimes a little harshly. The essay was, "My Room as a Reflection of My Personality." I've been assigning that essay for twenty years. First time anyone used the word "Mau Mau." Remember that Tom Wolfe book in the Sixties: *Mau Mauing the Flak Catchers*?

GEORGE

Can't say that I do, Ted.

TED

I did a little research about modern Kenya. There's a gang there that sees themselves as later-day Mau Maus. Most times the kids in my classes write stuff about things like the sports trophies they won as middle schoolers—to get a trophy, you just need to show up, apparently—or about a new x- box or how much they love their comforter. Charles mentions people's hands getting cut off with machetes.

GEORGE

Well, he didn't hold back, did he! Not to make light of it, my boy. You're right to take precautions, I see. We don't want another Virginia Tech. Or Columbine. Though technically, neither is a perfect analogy. But as I said, never a peep of a problem have we had. And any one we have had, was resolved.

(Ted takes a hold of the handle of his briefcase.)

TED

Oh? (Sets briefcase down again) In any case I appreciate your getting back to me here. I have to go. We meet in fifteen minutes. If I feel any threat, today, I'll be back in touch.

GEORGE

Yes, don't hesitate. It might be wise to keep your cell phone turned on. On vibrate of course. As this is not, apparently, a SOP situation–not routine.

TED

Will do. Thank you, sir.

GEORGE

George.

TED

Yes, George. I'll report back.

(The young woman reappears at the edge of the spotlight. George motions for her to come in).

GEORGE

No problemo. Thanks, Ted.

TED

Check. Bye.

(Ted is still standing next to the bench when Charles arrives. Ted releases the handle of his briefcase. Charles is a short, muscular fellow. He has backpack with him. He remains standing. He speaks with a colonial English accent. He is polite and formal, yet often brusque.

CHARLES

Professor.

TED

Charles.

(They awkwardly shake hands.)

TED

Wonder if they'll unlock our classroom door this time without me having to go to the office? I've had to complain before each class. They have only a single maintenance man, the secretary says, due to budget problems. "He doesn't unlock the door," I tell her. She looks at me, just shrugs. I'm tired of asking those math teachers. "I'll need to talk to the principal," I told her. "To Samuels." "You're welcome to," she said. I haven't done it yet, though.

CHARLES

The math teachers are nice enough about it.

TED

They have been, haven't they. Except for the drama teacher.

CHARLES

We're like orphans, man.

TED

Exactly. It's part of the general decline of education. Here we are at a high school. Part of the educational diaspora. You know that word?

CHARLES

Yes.

(Ted sits, and looks up at Charles.)

TED

Didn't mean to involve you in my problems. (More brightly) So how long have
you lived here, Charles?

CHARLES

You mean the States? Three years as of August.

TED

You mentioned family, in your essay.

CHARLES

What's left of it.

TED

Wars?

CHARLES

Yeah, ethnic rivalry. Also disease.

TED

I'm sorry to hear that, Charles.

CHARLES

And I just lost my job, even though I was the better worker of us two. Chris was
always wandering off for a smoke. But they couldn't afford two security guards.
He had a license. He was allowed to carry. They wanted someone who could carry. I carried, but I wasn't licensed to. I mean, man, it was a spooky place, just one
spotlight, like the face of a clock. Bleeding dark, I'm telling you. So the chickens
could sleep. A couple of guard dogs, Sam and Kevlar. Greyhounds. I mean, they
were his own pets. Garcia, the son of the bitch who fired me. Yesterday. No
notice either. Gave me my last paycheck. And then so long, beat it. Kumamako.

TED

What's that mean?

CHARLES (laughing)

Means "see you later alligator." In Swahili.

TED (smiling)

Your English is good.

CHARLES

My mother was a teacher in an English-speaking school. Middle school. My mother was a very smart woman.

TED

Sorry about the job, sounds hard. It's really tough out there lately. The Great Recession, but only for some. I lost two courses. I'm not protected like some others.

CHARLES

How's that, Professor Wilson?

TED

I didn't mean to talk about it.

CHARLES

I doubt mind.

TED

Anyway, you might not agree with me. It's about preference. I'm giving a face to it. "Affirmative Action," they call it. Anyway, it ruined my career. So here I am teaching a college class at a high school site... At least we have a small class—more attention to you guys, and not so many papers to grade, for me.

CHARLES

You didn't consider doing something else then?

TED

Good question. But my father was a professor. Engineering. And his father. English, like me. My older brother is an English professor. I wasn't going to be the first one not to be a professor. I tell people I went into the family business. It could be worse, I guess.

(The bell rings. The kids are heard filing out. Lya, in a low-cut top, passes by them.)

CHARLES

There are advantages to being at the high school. She's hot, man. Did they dress like that when you were in high school, Professor Wilson?

(Ted stands.)

TED (more professionally)

I better check the classroom. (But then turning back genially to Charles) I thought short-shorts were hot. Boy-shorts they call them now, I guess. But we didn't say "hot."

CHARLES

You said what, "Fine"? Or "Wassup, Holmes"?

(Ted laughs.)

TED

That was later, the 90's, I think. I have no idea who "Holmes" was. Unless it's Sherlock Holmes. We'd say "Cool." Or "she's a fox." Or, "she's totally third base," if she seemed...you know.

CHARLES

We wore uniforms to school. The girls culottes. A holdover from colonialism.

TED

Are they? I remember some yellow ones that Suzy... (Ted grabs his briefcase, thinking it's best not to continue.) Well, it's time. I bet our door is locked.

CHARLES (slinging his backpack over his shoulder)

I'm a little sympathetic—spent a lot of time myself locking things down. Securing things.

TED (starting forward but then stopping)

Weren't you afraid someone would discover your gun?

CHARLES

Chris probably knew about it, probably he told Garcia. I wouldn't put it past that pussy. Chris was two-faced, man. But even Chris couldn't have known for sure if I was packing. We had big pockets on our uniform.

TED (a bit taken aback, half-jokingly)

Glad you're not wearing a uniform.

CHARLES

Right, man. Parochial school was enough. No big pockets though. I was an altar boy. But the war broke out. AIDS did the rest, as I said. (angrily) All the fucking homosexuals.

TED

Charles, you can't talk like that around here. It's not acceptable.

CHARLES (quickly)

All right. Sorry, professor.

(Ted and Charles enter the school gates.)

TED (eyeing the student crowd)

I don't think students should wear uniforms. Not to school anyway. Maybe at home around the house.

(He smiles, charmed by his own joke.)

Scene Two

Two days later. Ted is sitting on bench outside of Cleveland High, again on the phone with George. George is seen in the back spotlight.

GEORGE

Just thought I'd touch base with you again, Ted, about your student. Don't want things to spin out of control. You know...

TED

I may have overreacted a bit, George. He continues to insist on being in the right. But he's engaged in the class. I think actually I can help him adjust. Must be weird suddenly finding yourself in a new world. There *was* one concerning moment. He came back late from our break–I give them ten minutes. Well, some of the kids were still hanging around the corridors, hitting on each other. Mostly boyfriend and girlfriend. You know what I mean, necking. If that's what they still call it. Half into to each other's clothes even.

GEORGE

You don't have to tell me, Ted. When I was a principal, we had to ban freaking. The school dances were like a group grope. I tell you, I couldn't believe my eyes.

TED

Know what you mean, George. Back-in-the day, some respect for women. Not a lot, but some at least. I'm pre-skate board, way before break dancing. There was a bit of elegance left. Tennis, not racketball. Skiing, not snowboarding. Know what I mean?

GEORGE

But they're not bad kids, not most of them anyway. They're just...

TED

Post-literate?

GEORGE (a bit taken aback)

"Hungry" was what I was going to say. But Ted, I just wanted to make sure you're doing all right there. Let you know you have institutional support, as I said. Want to come in and have chat with me, Ted? Just casual. I could pick your brains. Always interested in what's going on on the ground.

TED (to himself abstractly, not into phone)

Straight from dance to action, nothing in between. No conversation...nothing in the middle.

GEORGE

Ted?

TED (as if returning to familiar things)

Wish I had the time, George. For a chat. I spend three hours a day as a freeway flyer. Three days teaching. Two grading papers. Saturday's my day to get pissed.

GEORGE (trying not to react)

That only leaves Sunday, huh, doesn't it? That's the day I go to church, myself. Church and then football. A few beers for me, too, Ted. Don't think I don't understand. (He waits for Ted to speak, then) You single, my boy?

TED

And how. Divorced. She lives in Denver now. I think.

GEORGE

Not easy, is it? My wife died two years ago. Kids are up and grown, and off on their own. Kids, Ted? Don't mean to pry.

TED

Kids, not me. Just students. My ex was a former student.

GEORGE

Really.

TED

Yeah, I had a full-time position then.

GEORGE

How long ago was that?

TED

Ten years.

GEORGE

Tough times for sure.

TED

Damn straight. For some, at least.

GEORGE (tiptoeing around Ted's aggressiveness)

So what was it you were saying about what he was doing during the break? Your student?

TED

Oh, I don't know for sure. Thought he might be trying to chat up some of the high school girls. Seems pretty lonely. But I'm sure he's not a problem. Long as he's not packing. No metal detectors here, right?

(Ted stands, holding his briefcase. He takes out his sunglasses and puts them on. George, meanwhile, takes out a cigarette and lights it.)

George?

GEORGE

I'm here, Ted. I'm afraid there's no metal detectors, right. Cleveland is a pretty safe school in general. Core Magnet. Moderately upscale. Lots of Asians.

TED

Yeah, he was talking to an Oriental girl.

GEORGE

Was he? You mean, Korean?

TED

Or Cambodian. But if they're born here that makes them American, not Asians, right? No special designation is required.

(George shakes his head concernedly.)

Were you in Nam, George? During your military service. Hope you don't mind my asking.

GEORGE

Yes, I was there, sure was. As an officer.

TED

We're a funny generation, mine is—stuck between Vietnam and 9/11. Still searching for a language for that. But I've never even shot a gun myself. (Randomly) Except a BB gun. Shot my older brother's foot. Accidentally. ...But no metal detectors, right?

GEORGE

Well, if you think the boy—Charles, is it?—is carrying a weapon, it's best we address this through proper channels. Sooner than later. Good S.A. on your part, Ted.

TED

S.A.?

GEORGE

Situational awareness.

TED

I have no evidence. I'll find a way of finding out though. I've been teaching a long time.

GEORGE

Yes, you mentioned that.

TED

Seven states. Arizona, Massachusetts, Wyoming, Indiana—moved around as much as a serviceman. But I don't have a pension. Do you know some cops retire after twenty years at 90% pension? Some even double dip. Now that's what I call a union. Not us wandering scholars, mind you. California's got more prisons than schools. They keep throwing teachers in with cops and firefighters. I resent that, don't you, George? I never finished my dissertation, unfortunately. So maybe I have myself to blame. It was on NeoRomanticism. Henry Miller to...

GEORGE

Well, my boy, it's no problem for me to drop by Cleveland this week and sit down and have a chat with you. I certainly understand where you're coming from. I can't say I've exactly been in your shoes, but I've had a few challenges in my own life like anybody else. Maybe I could meet this young fellow, too. Just casually. Maybe sit in on a class. You can tell them you're being evaluated.

TED

Would that be the case?

GEORGE

Oh no, I mean just as a guise, Ted. I looked up your record. Exemplary. No problem there. It's just...

(The school bell rings.)

TED

The high school's letting out. No, it's not necessary right now, you coming here, George. A class is a delicate thing. I don't like to disrupt its flow, if possible. You know what I mean, right? A class is like a woman. You got to go easy—and then sometimes be firm. Ha.

GEORGE (sort of joining in)

Good you can keep your sense of humor about things in these bad times, Ted.

TED

Yeah, they're bad, aren't they. The cutbacks. I've been working in the fields a long time. Farming students.

GEORGE

Never quite thought of it that way, of course. It's the worse I've seen right now, no question. I consider myself lucky to have this lame...well, Ted, been good chatting with you. Wish I had more contact with instructors, but that's up to the department chair, you understand. They're territorial, too. But I'll stay in touch. I just want you to know you can call me, that...

TED

No need to bother, yet. But thanks for calling back, anyway.

GEORGE

Okay. Take care, Ted. I think I have someone on the other line.

(George puts his phone down. His secretary reappears at the edge of the spotlight. Meanwhile, students file out of the school.)

TED

I'm standing in a sea of teens right now. Bye, George. George?

Scene Three

Cleveland High School corridor. Ted arrives. Five students, including Charles, are standing outside F-1. Two Asian high school girls, Ji and Lya, stand together down the corridor.

TED (removing his sunglasses)

We're down to five? Sorry I'm late.

CHARLES

We were worried about you. (Then pointing to the two girls) Maybe we'll have to recruit some high school students for appearance sake.

(General laughter)

TED

We're okay. We still have a basketball team. Though if anyone gets injured we're in trouble. I guess I could be a player/coach. The other teachers are gone?

CHARLES

They wouldn't open for us.

STUDENT 1

We almost left. Carlos did leave. Fifteen minute rule, he said.

TED

The 405 was backed way up. (Half to himself) Some old, broken down—no doubt, unregistered—pickup truck holding up ten thousand lives.

CHARLES

Carlos.

(All but Student 2 laugh)

TED (realizing what has just happened)

Oh, I didn't mean...

STUDENT 2

Yes, it's not funny, Charles. I know Carlos. He would be the first one stop for someone if they were broken down somewhere.

TED

It was my bad.

CHARLES (to Ted)

Sorry. My mind's too quick for my bloody brain.

STUDENT 2 (to Ted)

Gloria called me and told me she couldn't be here today. Tried to contact you, she said.

TED

Forgot to turn my phone back on after I left the library. At least we have seven— provided everyone shows next time. Don't want them to cancel this class, do we? (He tries the door. It's locked.) The school is pretty cleared out. I'll need to go to the principal's office.

(Ted exits.)

STUDENT 1

Did you see his eyes? Bloodshot as a fish.

CHARLES

Maybe tired.

STUDENT 1

Yeah, maybe.

CHARLES

He's a good teacher. Give him a fucking break, man.

STUDENT 1 (challengingly)

I didn't say he wasn't a good teacher. What's it to you?

STUDENT 2

Boys, please!

(Ted returns.)

TED

You'd think if you work at a place, they'd give you a key, no? The principal is no-where to be found. The maintenance man is supposed to come, but I'm calling things off for today.

STUDENT 1

We could try some other doors, couldn't we?

CHARLES

Everything is locked.

TED (looking wonderingly at Charles, then to the others)

We'll pick up where we left off Wednesday. Hemingway and vocabulary. Sorry about this. At least you all live close by, right? See you next week. (randomly) The days are getting longer, aren't they? The reversible jacket of day turned inside out.

STUDENT 1 (sarcastically)

Poetic.

(Ted stares at Student 1 but doesn't react further.)

CHARLES (again, in Ted's defense)

No problem. See you on Monday, Professor.

(The others except Student 1 join in with byes.)

TED

See you. Sorry again. But enjoy the afternoon, guys.

(His students disperse. Ted stands before the door to F-1. He looks down the hall at the two girls, who are joking and laughing. He opens his briefcase, looks in, and then closes it back up. He turns to leave, but one of the girls, Ji, hurries down the hall to talk with him. She's Korean. Has long straight black hair. Is small and slim.)

JI

Sir?

(Ted turns around to look at her.)

TED

Me?

JI

Yes. Can I bother you?

(Ted checks to see if Lya is still there. Lya looks at the two of them. Waits for her friend.)

TED

Sure. No problem.

JI

That was your student?

TED

Which one?

JI

The black boy.

TED

Charles? Yes. Oh! You're the one...

JI

You saw us? He's been bothering me.

TED

I thought I saw something the other day. Today, too?

JI

My friend, Lya, was with me today. (Pointing) That's her. We stayed after to rehearse. But rehearsal was canceled. I'm waiting for my mom.

TED

The Importance of Being Earnest?

JI

How'd you know?

TED

What part do you play?

                              JI

Cecily.

                              TED (half-jokingly)

Is it an all-Asian production?

                              JI (looks at him skeptically)

No. Course not.

                              TED

So he didn't bother you today?

                              JI

Could I talk to you personal? Lya's my best friend, but so she can't hear—these corridors echo. You wouldn't believe the gossip. On Facebook and Twitter. Everywhere. Like acne.

                              TED

Oscar Wilde loved gossip.

                              (She laughs.)

We could use the classroom, but I'm locked out.

                              (Just at that moment, Dick, the maintenance
                              man, arrives. He grabs a chain of keys hang-
                              ing from his pants.)

                              DICK

You wanted in F-1? Sorry I wasn't here sooner. An incident in the parking lot. Two kids. Had to break up a fight. Hardly part of my job description. But I'm the only person on duty.

                              TED

I thought the principal stayed till four.

DICK

Samuels. Never. He moonlights as a coach. The guy's got two jobs. But I settled the argument. The usual gangbangers. Nothing compared to being in Iraq though. (Holding key up) No class today?

TED (looking at Ji)

We're...having individual conferences.

JI (quickly)

Yeah.

(Dick looks at her.)

DICK

You go here, right?

JI

I'm taking a college course.

DICK

Some of you types are pretty ambitious, I guess.

JI

Yeah.

DICK

This is a core magnet school. Did you know that, Mr ?

TED

Wilson.

DICK

Lots of smart ones. But we got some gangbangers, too.

(He unlocks the door.)

I'll leave it locked so all you have to do is pull it shut when you leave.

TED

Got you. I appreciate it.

DICK

I leave at 4:30.

(Dick exits. Ted holds the door for Ji. They enter. The lights are off, but, on a sensor, come on when they come in. They look at each other, smile.)

TED

When is your ride coming?

JI

Ten minutes.

(They sit down at two small wooden school desks next to each other.)

TED

Okay, shoot.

JI

He touched me.

TED

Not today?

JI

Today he just smiled at me. You know the smile boys give after they've done something.

TED

I guess.

JI

On Wednesday. After rehearsal. You saw us, right?

TED

I did, but I hoped it was innocent. Where'd he touch you, if I may ask?

JI (she hesitates)

On my breast.

TED

Both?

JI

The most reachable one. We were talking.

TED

You were?

JI

He was asking me stuff...I'm embarrassed. I come to you because he's your student.

(A pause. He eyes her quizzically.)

TED

What stuff?

JI

You know, first base, second base…and if I'd ever. (Bows her head) I haven't.

TED

Do you know the bases?

JI

Yeah.

TED

Is that what you told him, you hadn't?

JI

Yes.

TED

Why did you answer?

JI

I don't know.

TED

He may have found that encouraging.

JI

That I answered?

TED

Yes, and the other thing. That you haven't.

JI

I feel guilty. I haven't been able to sleep. Not even study. Like nada. I don't know half my lines. Whole speeches.

TED

But it wasn't accidental, right? I mean, his touching you. Not just brushing up against you, say.

JI

Oh, I'm sure. He was demonstrating second base.

TED

But what did he say?

JI (sort of into it)

When he did?

TED

Yeah. And about second base.

JI

He just laughed it off, like it was a joke, that he'd touched me. Like he was joking around. I don't remember what he said about second base.

TED

So you didn't object?

JI

I was shocked. I didn't know what to say or do. He hurried back to your class. You believe me, right?

TED

How'd he do it? If I'm to know what I'm talking about should I talk to him about it.

JI

Oh, I can't.

TED

Pretend you're in a play.

(She smiles. She stands, and rubs one breast with the back of her hand.)

JI (she shakes a little, a bit upset now)

Like that. It was first time for me.

(She sits again. He leans forward.)

TED

What do you want me to do? Report it? I think that's best.

JI

No. No. Please. I don't want to be famous around here.

TED

Then what? The principal, Samuels, should know.

JI

Not him! Not Principal Samuels. ...I don't want public.

TED

What is it that you want then?

(The lights go out.)

Should you move or me?

(She stands up and the lights come back on. Ted checks her out. She notices.)

JI (smoothing her shirt, self-conscious, yet flattered)

Sorry if I involve you.

TED

No, it's fine. I just don't know how I can help you, if you don't report it.

JI

Could you like just tell Charles I'm not into him? Keep an eye on him?

TED

I could do that, I suppose. You didn't do anything to make him think otherwise? About your intentions, I mean.

JI

No, I was totally surprised. He's got something in his head, I think.

TED

Ok. I'll talk to him about it.

JI

Thank you, sir. Professor Wilson?

TED

It's Ted.

JI

Thank you. You are a professor, right?

TED

Yes. English.

JI

I like English. I suck at math. I took freshman algebra in this room.

> (She stands, picks up a math book from a shelf, opens it, and then sets in on the desk she was sitting in. She sits once more.)

I feel better now. Having told you. But I need to go.

TED

Don't worry, I'll talk to him. And I won't involve others—Samuels or anyone—before talking to you first.

JI

Thank you, Professor...

TED

You're not my student.

JI

Okay, thank you...Ted. My mom is waiting.

TED

Then you should go.

> (She walks to the door, and then turns around toward him again.)

JI

I'm excited. My mom is taking me downtown this weekend to see a play. At the Forum.

TED

Oh. What play?

JI

By Euripedes. We read *The Glass Menagerie* in Advanced English. I want to play Laura!

TED

She's repressed.

JI

You mean, shy?

TED

Yes, I think you're right, more shy than repressed. It was a different time. Different era. More genteel. Polite. Formal.

JI

I can relate.

TED (half-jokingly)

Your mother is crazy?

JI (a bit taken aback)

What? Course not.

TED

Never mind. Just a joke. You can relate because?

JI

My mother's formal.

TED

Your father?

JI

He's back in Korea. They divorced.

TED

Oh, sorry. But I understand what you mean. There's a novel I sometimes teach: *The Good Soldier.* Some of my Hispanic students can relate because their father is macho. And formal. The classics are always best. (Ted starts to rise but remains sitting.) Maybe I'll meet your mother someday. Never know.

JI

You like?

(She edges toward the door.)

But she will kill me if I make her wait. She'll think I'm up to something. She doesn't want me in this play. She's afraid I'll meet wrong people.

TED

Have a good weekend.

JI

Okay. Have a good one yourself, Professor...Ted.

TED

What's your name?

JI

Ji. Bye.

TED

Okay, bye Ji.

(She exits. Ted doesn't move. He sits there for a while. The lights go out, though there is still a faint light from the classroom windows. Ted reaches into his briefcase, pulls out

(a silver flask, and drinks, causing the lights to come on again. He reaches for the math textbook on the desk Ji sat at. He doesn't notice Charles who we now see is peering in at him from one of the windows. Ted is reading aloud.)

TED

An angle is formed by two rays that have the same endpoint. That point is called the vertex; the rays are called the sides of the angle. An angle is formed by rays AB and AC. A is the vertex. AB and AC are the sides of the angle. The angle can be named by the letters of the three points that form it—therefore the angle in Figure 16 could be named angle BAC or angle CAB. The center letter is always the letter of the...

(There is a knock at the door. He jumps halfway out of his seat.)

TED

Shit!

(He screws the top on the flask and replaces it in his briefcase. Then walks to the door and opens it. Charles stands there.)

Oh, Charles. You startled me.

(Charles enters with backpack. They remain standing.)

CHARLES (mock innocently)

Who did you think it might be?

TED

The maintenance man.

CHARLES

He's gone. I saw him go.

TED (trying to appear offhand)

You've been hanging around all this time?

CHARLES

I forgot my backpack. Had to climb the bleeding fence to get in.

TED

I was just leaving. (Walking over to the same desk and picking up the math book) I got caught up reading this math textbook. Took me back to school days. I haven't sat in a student's desk in a long while–a different perspective. I was a whiz at algebra but not so good at geometry. An ex- girlfriend, a math major, said, "Geometry is deduction and you're so logical, Ted." I don't think I had maybe the visual sense for geometry. I got caught cheating on a geometry exam when I was a high school sophomore. I shouldn't tell you that, huh? Why I am, I don't know. Fortunately, we were moving that summer. Out here. So they agreed it wouldn't be part of my permanent record. The cheating part. I got an "F" in geometry and had to take it over at my new school. My geometry teacher at the new school wanted to move me into the advanced class because my geometry skills were ahead of the class at the beginning. But I said, "No," I'll stay in this class. She was surprised by my answer. But I knew that as the semester continued I'd sink back to a more normal level. I got a "B" in the class.

CHARLES

You wound up in Literature.

(Ted sits down at the same desk as before.)

TED

Yes, so I guess it doesn't matter. But you know how you always go back to things. (Gesturing to Charles) Want to sit?

CHARLES

I'm fine. (But then sits, in the desk Ji was in) How did you get so good at English?

TED

Just practice. Going over things. But we all miss things. I worked a year on Whitman's poem "Song of Myself," where it goes, "A child said *What is the grass? fetching it to me with full hands; How could I answer the child? I do not know what it is any more than he*" —and it goes on. But I worked on that section for weeks without realizing that there were two questions not one. That was sort of humiliating.

(Charles rises, paces.)

CHARLES

I go back to the war. I have terrible thoughts in my head sometimes.

TED (self-focused)

I suppose my tribulations are minor. But they eat at me. One goes back to humiliations, and to the times one cheated. (More directly to Charles) Not to mention, *being* cheated. Those, too. The sense of being had.

CHARLES

Could I have a drink?

TED (feigning)

A drink?

CHARLES

I saw you through the windows.

                    TED

You were watching?

                    CHARLES

Just for a few minutes.

                    TED (forced casualness)

Oh. When did you return?

                    CHARLES

Why?

                    TED (covering)

Just curious. Are we locked in? I'll need to climb the fence to get to my car? Not very professional, is it? Is there really no one else here?

                    CHARLES

I guess not. It's past five.

                    TED

Already.

                    CHARLES

Look out the windows.

                    (Ted turns to look.)

                    TED

I see what you mean. Black as charred wood.

                    (Charles is a bit taken aback by the simile,
                    but says nothing. He sits in a different desk.)

CHARLES

I need a drink.

TED

If we were caught on school property...

> (Ted opens his briefcase, glances around, and takes out the flask.)

I'd be fucked.

> (He hands the flask to Charles, who drinks.)

CHARLES

You can trust me, Professor Wilson. This reminds me of working nights at the chicken farm with Chris.

TED

You found your backpack?

CHARLES

In the hallway.

TED

I didn't notice it.

CHARLES

Were you distracted?

TED

Distracted?

CHARLES

They're cute, eh, man?

TED

Who are?

(Charles drinks again from the flask, sets it
down. Ted takes the flask back and puts it
on his desk.)

CHARLES

Don't worry, I'm on my bike. I don't have a car.

TED

Two snorts is enough. I am driving, but I haven't had much. Locked in? You'd
think the maintenance man would have noticed my car in the lot. ... What is
cute?

CHARLES

I saw you looking at them, earlier. I saw that you saw me talking to one of
them…in the hallway. One of the Asian ones. You saw me the other day, right?
During the break, Wednesday?

TED

Yes, I did. What's up with that?

CHARLES

I like her. What do you think I should do? I don't know my way away around
girls in America. I had a girlfriend for a while but she said we were incompatible.

TED

What did she mean?

CHARLES

I don't know. She said, "Dude, the cultural difference is too strong." I get the
same thing from blacks here. Africans don't fit in with African-Americans. Isn't
that bleeding…bleeding something. I wouldn't know how to say it here.

TED

Bleeding rich, perhaps...like me being locked in here.

CHARLES

Just now I watched the Korean girl—she won't tell me her name—get in her mom's car after rehearsal. I guess it wasn't locked yet. She told me the other day that she was in a play. She told me that much. And some other things. (He grabs the flask off Ted's desk. Drinks.) Why do you drink, professor?

TED

Don't assume I'm drunk, I'm not, I told you. But you can have the rest. I've had enough. I drink...? I guess because I'm not one of the "swells." My mother used to speak of the "swells." The privileged.

CHARLES

The rich?

TED

Those born to it.

CHARLES

That's all. Nothing deeper. A mental disorder of some sort?

TED

I beg your pardon? (yet amused) Like?

CHARLES

Homosexuality.

TED

Not that I know of. Anyway, we no longer consider that a mental disorder.

CHARLES

90% of suicides have a mental disorder. Other factors, like an economic down-turn, push them over the edge, said my psych professor. In my country we kill "homosexuals." It's a filthy word. Any kind of butt sex is illegal.

TED

Yeah, I got the impression earlier you don't like them, it. Me, I don't like any group as a group. When I lived in Boston, I disliked the Irish. And I myself am a quarter Irish. I always tell people I'm fortunate to be a quarter Irish.

CHARLES (smiling)

I get it.

TED

But if I commit suicide it's because I'm not one of the swells. That's my sto-ry and I'm sticking to it. (Leans in) I've got something to discuss with you, Charles?

CHARLES

Go ahead, man.

TED

But first, just to be clear—you're not suicidal, are you? I mean I can get you help, through the college, if you need it. Just someone to talk to. I want you to know you have the resources of the college behind you. Institutional support. You aren't, right, suicidal or anything?

CHARLES

Not that I know of. And I'm talking to you. I'm just horny, that's all.

TED (a bit manically)

Horny is good. Horny is fuel. We need fuel to keep going. Besides, a writer—I used to think of myself as one of those—needs something wrong with him. Or have wrongness thrust upon him. But it's possible to be too wrong, or wronged. But, speaking of fuel, what I really what to ask...

CHARLES

I have something to ask you, sir.

TED

You do? Shoot.

CHARLES

You know how on my first paper you warned me about guns. I love guns, but I appreciated that, the advice. What I want to know is, do you think I'm a good writer? I fill reams of notebooks with words. I don't call myself a writer, but some day I'd like to be, I think.

TED

As I said, writers are horny, there's that. I've read enough literary biographies. But if you're asking me, could you be a writer? I don't know. It's not for me to say. I thought your first essay was really good. Really descriptive. It had the feel of a writer.

CHARLES

Wow, that's cool to hear. Don't worry, I would never tell on you, Professor Wilson. I've got your back. Is that how to say it?

TED (more teacherly)

Yes. Thanks. But lay off the girl, okay? There are penalties if you did something. You might get deported for one thing. She's only fifteen or so. You're twenty, right? You can't date her. If you were eighteen you'd be within the law. But anyway girls here own their own bodies. You can't do anything without their consent.

CHARLES

What if she's incapacitated?

TED (jerking his head)

What? I hope you're fucking kidding.

CHARLES

I mean, no one owns their bloody body absolutely. There are exceptions, right? You can't walk around with no clothes on. You can't put certain drugs in your body.

TED

Ah, ok, if that's what you meant. That's very Socratic of you. But let's keep to the issue at hand.

(Charles rises.)

CHARLES

Did she say something to you?

TED (challengingly)

As a matter of fact, she did. She wanted me to say something to you. Said you touched her. Her breast.

CHARLES

That was nothing.

TED

She didn't think so. Girls are different. They think nothing is something. But in this case, I wouldn't call it nothing.

CHARLES

Whose side are you on? Dude, you get me to open up and all this time you're playing me?

TED (rising from the desk)

Listen, she asked me to talk to you. Diffuse the situation. As it is, I'm going outside channels. Anything else happens, I won't hesitate to report you. As of now, she's not going to press the issue as long as you lay off.

CHARLES

I like her. I was just goofing her.

TED

Get real. You barely know her. She likable, yeah. She's cute. But she's only fifteen. A virgin.

CHARLES

How you know that? She told you? You getting personal with her? She's mine.

TED (staring out the windows)

I wouldn't dream of it. (Turning back to Charles) But she's not yours, Charles. I don't know what it's like where you come from, but it doesn't work that way here.

CHARLES

Listen, man, I'm giving you fair warning because I like you, and respect you as a teacher. I'm going to have that girl, if she'll have me. And I'm telling you, you interfere I'll mention our little drink.

TED

Your word against mine? And they'd throw you out, too, if they believed you. I'm telling *you*, next time she'll complain to the authorities. I'm saving your ass, here.

CHARLES

She likes me, I'm telling you.

TED (marveling)

How do you know that, Charles?

CHARLES

She told me.

TED

When?

CHARLES

The first time, when you weren't there. Two weeks ago.

TED (half to himself)

She didn't mention a first time. (then directly) What did she say to make you think such a thing? That she was receptive?

CHARLES

She said I was handsome. She said I had beautiful black skin. Like black sand, she said. She put her arm next to mine. Said yellow and black go well together. She *is* a bit yellow. They have a tinge these Asian girls.

TED

Doesn't mean she likes you, even if she was flirting. Girls flirt. They like to draw attention, exhibit themselves. It's the thing they like most. The thing they've been encouraged to do. Think about their body.

(Charles drinks the last of the whiskey, shaking the bottle to indicate it's empty.)

CHARLES

She's in that play, right, man? I'm going to see it and you can't stop me. Next week. Here at the high school. Two nights. I'm going to be there both nights. She'll see me there, watching her. She'll understand what I'm saying. My intentions are honorable. My father never taught me honor, but my mother did. And just so you know, I'm going to keep coming to class, too, so I've got an excuse to see her. I don't want to quit this course, anyway. I want to be that writer I spoke of. But I'll leave her alone until the play. But there's one thing you need to do, professor.

TED

What's that?

CHARLES

Not bloody give me away.

TED

Meaning what?

CHARLES

Don't tell her I'm coming to the play. She could get me barred or something.
Or maybe that friend of hers might tattle-tell on me. I don't want to upset
her before her performance or anything anyway, I just want to be there. If
she won't have me, after that I'll leave her alone. Maybe I shouldn't have
touched her. But her breast was right there, inches away. Part of it was already showing. Parts of both of them. I made a joke of it, so she wouldn't
feel creeped out.

TED

Well, she was anyway, creeped out. (He walks toward the windows and turns
back to Charles.) But if you promise, Charles—both, not to bother her and accept
the verdict...

CHARLES

That's between me and my confessor, professor—just remember, your job's at
stake.

TED

Don't threaten me, Charles. You don't know who you are dealing with.

CHARLES

Okay, I promise. I don't want to hurt her. I don't want to hurt you either, but
you understand, don't you? What it's like to be alone, struggling to survive?
Drowning in memories?

(Charles grabs his backpack.)

And humiliations?

TED

I was about to say, if you'd given me a chance and if you're serious, as you say you are, then I'll see what I might do to help you. With her. If she's into it, as you claim.

CHARLES

You would? Why?

TED

Because I understand your feelings. And I, too, wanted to be a writer. She's your muse, I guess. Or your first one. I think that's what's going on here. I had one once just like her. Sort of. But I'll tell you something, Charles: I screwed up that romance but acting impulsively. She was a real girl not just a muse. Still, I give those who want to write a special dispensation. A pass. Maybe I shouldn't, but I do, up to a point. I'm willing to help you. But, as I said, only if she's into it. Otherwise, I'll see that she reports you.

CHARLES

Okay, I can be patient. But I hope you're not messing with me, professor. I'm not a blinking fool. I don't trust people, you know. I've seen too much. But I'm going to trust you for now because I like you. And like I said you're a good teacher.

TED (cooly)

Okay, I'll see you Monday then, Charles. Leave it to me, remember. Don't go near her.

CHARLES

All right, cool. (He moves to the door, turns around, and smiles.) I get so horny just thinking about her.

(Ted stares at him. Charles exits. Ted sits down again, numbly. He looks out the windows and then at his watch.)

BLACKOUT

END OF ACT ONE

Act Two

Scene Four

The stone bench outside the locked high school gates. Ted is sitting. Charles arrives, unseen at first by Ted. Charles remains standing.

TED

Don't sneak up on a person like that.

CHARLES

African veldt training. Did you think I'd dropped?

TED (laughing)

I was half hoping you did.

(Ted's cell phone rings. He looks at the number.)

Sorry, I need to take this, Charles. I'll see you inside.

(He gets up and walks a few paces away from Charles. Charles sits on the stone bench, opens a paperback, and reads.)

Hello.

GEORGE (in spotlight)

It's George, Ted. How are you?

TED

Fine. Fine. No issues.

GEORGE

Good. But I had a report, I'm afraid.

TED (fearfully)

You did?

GEORGE

Yes, Ted. A security camera caught you climbing over the fence at Cleveland at 17.5 hours Friday.

TED

Oh that.

GEORGE

The camera only caught you as you were climbing out, so I'm sure there's a perfectly reasonable explanation, Ted, but it's something I'm required to check into. Samuels wanted me to, too. Procedure, you understand.

TED

I was locked in.

GEORGE

You were still there after class?

TED

Yes. I thought you said Dick left at five.

GEORGE

Dick? Oh, you mean the janitor. Supposed to be five. That's my understanding. But it was even after five when the camera caught you.

TED

I couldn't find an exit.

(The school bell rings. Ted turns around to
see Charles entering the gates.)

I'm going to have to go, George. Sorry. School's letting out. I was working on
something in the classroom Friday and lost track of the time. I do apologize.
Don't know what I was thinking. Didn't occur to me that I wouldn't be able to
get out. That I was locked in. When I went to high school there were no fences.
But it won't happen again, I assure you.

GEORGE

I understand, Ted. Things like this happen, occasionally. But I'll need to come
by the school and talk to you and have you sign my report before I pass it on
to Samuels. Today good? Give me a chance to see your problem student, too,
maybe.

TED

Today's not so good, no. But how about Wednesday? Soon enough? Before class,
say. I'll be on the stone bench next to the gates. Charles, the student, is usually
there at that time, too. He's calmed down, though. I'm not concerned anymore.
He's really a very talented kid...

GEORGE

Good to hear that. Wednesday...

TED

Beats the heck out of most of them.

GEORGE

Don't say. Well, Wednesday then. I'll be seeing you then, there, okay? If anything changes, I'll call you. Have a good session, Ted. You've got an excellent
reputation as a teacher, I understand. The chair, Barbara, thinks highly of you.
She seems to think you're some sort of genius or something, my boy. Got a sense
she likes you. There are a lot of fish in the sea, Ted. All kinds of fish. Know what

I mean. Don't get discouraged. We don't want anything bad, checkered, on your record. This is no time to be looking for a job. Don't worry, we'll clear this thing up. See you Wednesday.

(The spotlight goes off. Ted shuts off phone and sits back down resignedly on the bench. At last he rises and enters the school. Ji is standing next to the gates.)

JI

Hi, sir.

TED

Okay, we'll stick with that.

JI

Huh?

TED

Yes "Ted" is probably not a good idea.

JI

Oh, sorry, I forgot.

TED

How about "Sensei"?

JI (smiling)

We hate Japanese.

(Ted laughs hollowly.)

TED (starting to leave)

I'm afraid I have class now.

                              JI

I saw them go in. Charles, too.

                              TED

You spoke with him?

                              JI

No. Did you?

                              TED

Yes. But I must go.

                              JI

Me, too. Eat and do homework before dress rehearsal tonight.

                              TED (warming to her)

Dress rehearsal. Exciting. Break a leg.

                              JI

Want to come? It's open to the public.

                              TED

Oh, I can't. Won't your mother be there? Siblings?

                              JI

Just have a little brother. Mom will be home with him. I'm nervous about tonight.

                              TED

What time is the rehearsal?

                              JI

She'll drop me off at six. Rehearsal at six-thirty. You come at six we could talk. I want to know what Charles said. Can't you?

TED

Here?

JI

Yes, no problem, it will be dark. (Pointing) "See that dear old tree there"–that's one of Cicely's lines.

TED

Handy. You've learned your lines then?

JI

My mother drill me. I understand if you can't come.

TED

I have an engagement. I'll be seeing the actual performance though.

JI

What kind? Can I ask?

TED

What kind what?

JI

Engagement. Sorry if I'm too curious.

TED

Nothing secret. I'm on a softball team.

JI

I like baseball. You are good?

TED

In high school I was. The softball team is more like a drinking club.

JI

It's good you have activity. Drama is mine. (She fidgets with her hair.) I have to go now, too.

(He looks at the tree.)

TED

I guess I could swing by at six. We should talk, yes. I'm a little worried about Charles. I'll be here.

JI

Okey. Dokey. I just learn that. Not Japanese. Bye.

(She runs off. Then he exits.)

Scene Five

In the classroom. Four students, including Charles, sit at school desks in a small circle. Charles is quiet while the other three chat. There are three empty desks in the circle. Ted enters. He sits at one of the desks.

TED

Hi. Sorry to be late. (He looks at the two empty desks, then...) We few, the brave.

CHARLES

Do we have a quorum?

TED

Um? Maybe a *four*-um. ...and I'm the *um* pire.

(Laughter)

Speaking of vocabulary, let's do that second today. First Hemingway—a sportsman himself. Okay, Hemingway's on first...remember "Say-heh Willie Mays?"

(More laughter)

No, I suppose you don't. (He looks out the window.) "A Clean, Well-Lighted Place." Page thirteen.

(Ted reads aloud.)

"Last week he tried to commit suicide," the one waiter said. Which waiter?

STUDENT 1

The younger.

TED

Yeah. (reading) "Why?" "He was in despair." "What about?" "Nothing." "What" is a key word in this story. Hemingway chooses a few words and riffs on them. He comes back to "nothing" when we get to "nada." The prayer riff on "Our Father." (reading) "What about?" "Nothing." "The guard will pick him up."

STUDENT 1

The older.

TED

Right. (reading) "What does it matter if he gets what he's after?" The younger. You hear it, two "what's."

CHARLES

What's the point?

(Laughter)

TED

Well, it's journalistic for starters. Who? What? When? Why? And How? Hemingway started as a journalist. And it's like a detective story. And then, existential. What's it all about? Life, that is. Questions. "What did he want to kill himself for?" "Who cut him down?" "His niece." "His niece," an odd piece of information. But it tells us he has relations. There's a lot of "w" sounds. "What?"

"Why?" etc. Also the sound of "want" playing off "what." "I want to go to bed." That's the young one. "What is an hour?" And a funny one comes at the end. "'What's yours?' asked the barman." That's sexual. The same question is asked at the beginning of his story "The Killers." There's always this murky sexuality in Hemingway. "What's yours?" I'll show you mine if you show me yours.

> (Laughter, but a bit uncomfortable. The students look at each other wondering about Ted.)

"What's yours?" Behind it we hear, "How's yours?"

CHARLES

Fine.

> (Laughter)

STUDENT 2

Boys!

STUDENT 1

What is this thing you're doing called. It's freaky.

TED

Which?

CHARLES

It's breaking things down. It's child's play.

TED (looking critically at Charles)

No, it's explication. Teasing out meanings.

CHARLES

I was just trying to help. (Smiling, pointing to Student 1) Him.

STUDENT 1

I can speak for myself, Charles.

CHARLES

Go right ahead then, man.

TED (seeking to mollify the situation)

Yeah, one might ask, as Beckett does somewhere, "What does it matter who is speaking?"

STUDENT 1 (angrily)

I say it matters.

TED

I'm with you on that one. I suspect Charles is, too, though I hesitate to speak for him. His experiences aren't mine. It, speaking, has to do with power, right? And position in life. Whether one is a younger waiter or an older waiter, for example. But the younger waiter will someday be old, and the older was once young, like the younger waiter, so it's not fixed or final, one's position. Yet maybe the difference has less to do with age in that case than with temperament. The older waiter says to the younger: "We are two different kinds." The older waiter is passive and the younger active. To be active is to be stupid. Americans are stupid because we believe we control our own destiny.

STUDENT 1

The story is set in Spain, professor. They're Spanish.

TED

True. And Hemingway an exile.

CHARLES (challengingly)

I think they're just different. Being old—and passive—is not being right. Or smart.

TED (cooly)

Well, you two appear to agree then. About that at least. "Different" and "difference" are words we often come across in Hemingway. But speaking of words, we should do our vocabulary.

STUDENT 2

But what's the story about, Professor Wilson? Loneliness?

(She is a small, attractive girl. Ted eyes her, smiles.)

TED (almost romantically)

Nothingness, I think. Loneliness is a feeling, but nothingness is something we know, Hemingway suggests. He's always interested in feeling something vs. knowing something. He's on the side of knowing. But knowing on a primal level. Deep in your solar plexus.

STUDENT 2

How can you know nothingness though?

TED

Good question. But I wouldn't want to get lost in semantics. Words. (He stares out the window.) Somehow we know it, he suggests. It goes off in your hand. (Looking back at the students) But speaking of words–did I already say that?– let's indeed do vocabulary.

(Ted and the students open their vocabulary texts.)

Page forty-five. Charles? Would you begin? Exercise 1.

CHARLES (quietly angry)

Just the answers, or the sentences, too, sir?

TED

The answers, Charles.

CHARLES (reading)

Adversary. Obverse. Inadvertent. Introvert. Averse. (slight pause) Perverse. (then) Converts...

(His voice continues as lights dim. In the half-dark, we see Ted standing under a tree, alone. There's a spotlight, from the school building. Ji enters.)

JI

Sorry I'm late. My mother.

TED

I saw them. Your younger brother is how old?

JI

Ten. He's totally annoying. He gets all the attention of course. Old school Korean.

TED

Must be different, a triangle, no father there.

JI

Lots of kids these days have same.

TED

Yes, I know. My parents stayed together for "the children," as we say. Your mother's attractive...like her daughter.

JI (pleased)

Thank you, professor...okay, I try "Ted." I never speak to adult first name. (She giggles, then) If close friend of family, we say "Uncle," then name. You have children, Ted? Sorry if I pry more.

TED

It's okay. I pried first. No, no kids. Just didn't happen somehow. I've been married twice though.

JI

Third time is charm maybe. This is a wishing tree. That's what students say.

TED

That is charming. I know I can have kids though, there was one time.... Well, never mind that. Sometimes I do wish I had children. Especially a girl-child. I grew up in a family of all boys. Six boys. My parents kept trying for a girl. I would have liked to have a sister. To know what that's like. (He picks a leaf off the ground.) The trees are turning. I was driving yesterday down a street that had a bunch of yellows and reds. Made me wish for childhood–lots of red maples where I grew up. Down by the river, the colors were brilliant in the fall. (randomly) But not the brightest red I've ever seen. In high school, I remember looking at slides of blood in the microscope. I wonder where they got the blood? Have you had biology yet?

JI

I take it next year. (Withdrawing a bit, now that she's drawn out Ted) Mr. Stieglitz would be mad if I were late.

TED (returning to the present)

The drama teacher. The territorial one.

JI (not getting reference)

He doesn't like tardy. He has cute way with kids though.

TED

Cute?

JI

Teasing way.

TED

Not important and earnest like me.

(She laughs.)

JI

He's gay, we think.

TED

Oh, that's why he's territorial.

JI

What?

TED

Oh, nothing. You'll find out soon enough if you pursue theater.

JI

I thought lonely. Now I think bitter.

TED (laughing)

Yes, smarty pants, maybe you're right. I don't know the difference any-more–if I ever did. Especially when I've had a couple. Anyway, maybe it's the teacher in him not the gay in him that makes him territorial. (as if returning to familiar things) My father taught science, first in high school and later at a college. He went back for his Ph.D. at forty. I loved high school, myself.

JI (a bit uncomfortable)

It's okay, sometimes. Now I have friends. Before I felt trapped. I was looking for a friend.

TED (half to himself)

It's its own world, isn't it? Its own territory, if you will. Well, sometimes it feels like a prison, yes, you're right. High school. But one was a complete person then with a complete social network: a girlfriend, friends, teammates–a variety of classes and teachers. And each year you moved forward with your group to more exciting prospects: varsity, advanced placement, sex, road trips, keggers at the river, acquiring opinions. I was editor of the newspaper. Actual sex. Even the SAT was exciting in its way. Sitting in a big room with a bunch of your class-mates, not talking, scribbling your answers. Do you realize what you have, Ji? Youth, beauty, a social network. Charm. Youth is so charming. So glamourous. Everything disproportional. Everything mattering so. It's like a disease. A social disease. Like in *West Side Story*. You know that musical? I had a purple shirt like Bernardo, one of the Sharks...the PR's.

JI

What? Who? You lost me, Ted. What's that's short for?

TED

Theodore.

JI

No, I mean PR's.

TED (drifting)

Oh, Puerto Ricans. I read recently that they are the lowest economic group in all of New York City. Lower than African-Americans. They're all fighting over a small pie anyway, that's why they hate each other. I had a girl student once, Russian. Nice, very smart. If my students are any measure, the Russians are maybe the smartest people in the world–if not,well, well-balanced. One time she said, "Everybody hates the Armenians." Just like that. Couldn't believe what I was hearing from her sweet mouth. I expect Charles has seen a lot of hate. Just think of vampires. They've been around so long, no wonder they are not friendly.

JI (happy to get back to the immediate)

Did you talk to Charles? He didn't bother me today. I saw him looking though.

TED (cooly)

That's legal.

JI (almost cheerfully)

I guess. I was looking, too. Hard to keep your eyes off him. We don't have black people in Korea. He's handsome. And so black. Like nighttime.

TED

You like him? I'm jealous.

JI (perplexed)

You mean it? ...Oh, you're just teasing. Like Mr. Stieglitz. I like looking at Charles, I guess. Is that shame?

(She lowers her head. An awkward pause.)

TED

He wants to come to your play this weekend. Wanted me to ask you if it was okay?

JI

He's being polite? A little late, fool.

TED

He's not a bad kid, I think. Boys his age don't always demonstrate self-control, believe me.

JI

He's what, twenty? Why you defend him?

TED

He's at his sexual peak. You'll get there when you're thirty.

JI (enthusiastic)

Really? But I think adolescence must be sexual peak. Everybody here makes sex jokes all the time.

TED

Mostly boys, I expect. Boys at eighteen hit their sexual peak. Females, thirty. That's what they say, anyway.

JI

Something to look forward to after *my* Ph.D.

(She leans back against the tree.)

Just joke. My mom says Ph.D. is highest. Highest is best. You have Ph.D.?

TED

I didn't finish it. Didn't finish my dissertation, "Neo-Romanticism: Henry Miller to Early Ashbery."

JI

That's a funny first name, "Early." Are they writers?

TED

Yes. Romantic self-disgust is the theme. I like to say the dissertation title aloud, for fun. Sometimes when I'm drinking in my apartment, I say it aloud a few times. I have a mirror next to the recliner, so I say it into the mirror. The mirror is also next to the TV, so it catches my minute reactions to the TV shows, too. I keep my TV running.

JI

Oh. Then you are lonely?

TED

I suppose. Are you?

JI (straightening up some)

I have school.

TED

And rehearsal.

JI

Yeah. In a few minutes.

TED

In a play you always know who's speaking?

JI

What?

TED

Sometimes in a story, especially in Hemingway's stories...you know him?

JI

The Old Man and the Sea? We read that last year. I loved.

TED

Well sometimes in his work you can't tell who's speaking. He even leaves out "He said" or "She said."

JI

I remember.

TED

But I'm going off again. Is it all right with you if Charles comes to your play? I think it's the best way to defuse the situation.

JI

He's wants? I guess it's okay, if you come, too. If you're there... to protect me.

TED

Oh I'm sure you'll be safe enough. I don't imagine he's actually a violent kid though he saw a lot of violence, in Africa, he said. And, presently, he's out of a job. He wants to come both nights.

JI (almost gleefully)

That's weird. I think maybe he's possessed with me.

TED

He said he just wanted to watch you, that's all. That's what he wants, just watching, I guess.

JI

Just that?

TED

That's what he said. But you could still report him. I'd back you up.

JI

Would you?

TED

But it's better if you report it yourself.

JI

I don't want trouble. Not Korean way. (looking away) He can come. But you'll come too, both nights, right?

TED

Sure. I look forward to it. It's a funny play. And further, I'm looking forward to seeing you in it.

JI (flattered and curious)

You are?

TED

Yes, of course. I feel this connection with you. Don't know why exactly, but I know I do...

JI

I feel same way...

TED (overlapping)

...even if I shouldn't.

JI

I don't worry.

TED

No? Okay. (Archly) You're very self possessed, composed, for a...youngster.

JI (smiling)

See you Friday then. I won't be at school Wednesday. It's my birthday.

TED

Really? How old?

JI

Sixteen. My mother is taking me to get my driver's license. First time she's ever allowed me to miss school.

> TED

Wow, this is a big week for you.

> JI (she fidgets with hair)

Yes, meeting you, too.

> TED

Thanks. (It appears as though he wants to touch her, but he resists and instead touches the bark of the tree.) Charles will wonder where you are Wednesday.

> JI

What will you tell him?

> TED

That you're preparing, studying your lines. I was in a play only one time. I played Malcolm in Shakespeare's *Macbeth*.

> JI

I read it last year.

> TED

I became king and retired from acting.

> JI

I had nightmares.

> TED

Yes, she bullies him, and he's no picnic in any case.

> (Ji smiles, but then looks toward the school.)

JI

I must totally go.

TED

So I tell him it's okay for him to attend? It's your call.

JI

Is there a way to stop him?

TED

I suppose not really. Except report him. He seems to want your permission. I'm afraid he sees himself as your suitor.

JI

Suitor?

TED

Knight in shining armor.

JI

Okay, if you think, okay. You'll be there. Would you like to sit with my mother and brother? I have three comps. Each night. She's coming both nights.

TED

Sure. I'd like that. Get to know the family of the star.

JI

Haha. You're funny... Theodore. Bye. Don't be lonely!

TED

Okay. Thanks.

(Ji exits. Ted remains standing under the tree. He moves out of the spotlight.)

Scene Six

The stone bench. There is the sound of wind. The tree rustles. Ted is alone. He looks around expectantly. George enters. Unlike Ted, who is dressed casual, George is wearing a suit. He has white hair, cut short. He holds his cell phone in his right hand.

GEORGE

You must be Ted? Sorry we haven't met before now.

(Ted rises. The men shake hands.)

TED

Nice to meet you, George. Have a seat? I've started to think of this as my bench.

GEORGE

Thanks.

(They sit, both faced forward.)

We still have a few minutes before your class, right?

TED (a bit apprehensive)

Yes.

GEORGE

No sign of...Charles is it?

TED

He's usually here by now. Likes to chat me up. Seems to need a friend, or mentor. Wants to be a writer, he says. He's got some talent.

GEORGE

So you said…. you a writer yourself, Ted?

TED

Once upon a time, a long time ago. I enjoy seeing Charles spread his wings. Well, I enjoy it and don't enjoy it. Get a bit envious.

> (George glances at his cell phone and then puts it in his pocket.)

GEORGE

Sorry I may not get a chance to meet the young man.

TED

You brought the report? I apologize again.

GEORGE

There's one thing I want to clear up before I submit it to Samuels. He's a bit of a stickler for details.

TED

Shoot.

> (George side-eyes Ted. Then turns sideways in order to speak to Ted more directly.)

GEORGE

Well, I spoke with Dick, the janitor fellow on my way in. I want to come straight to the point, Ted. He said you met with some girl, some "Asian girl," he said, last Friday in the room. Alone. He said the class apparently was canceled that day.

TED

Yes, it was. I was frustrated by the school's inability to remember to open the door. I've asked them maybe half a dozen times, but they can't seem to get it together. I lost my cool, I guess. Told the students to go home. That I was going to have a chat with the principal.

GEORGE

I understand your frustration, Ted. I'm certainly going to discuss this with Samuels today. He didn't mention any discussion with you.

TED

Well, just at that moment that Dick fellow arrived. And Ji—this girl you refer to—wanted to talk with me. It was she who came to me. So I thought we might as well use the room. Her mom was waiting. It was for only a few minutes.

GEORGE

Is she one of ours, Ted? She's in the class?

TED

No. She's the one I told you about, the high school kid that Charles had come on to. I told her I'd speak with Charles. I told her I'd clear things up. Tell Charles the attentions weren't wanted. Weren't reciprocated. Or to report it to Samuels, I told her. She didn't want to do that, however.

GEORGE

I knew there was a reasonable explanation, Ted. I know you wouldn't do something untoward. But I wish you would have mentioned it originally. And I'm not sure this is something you should involve yourself in, you know, play go-between. (He eyes Ted closely.) The girl is satisfied? You are?

TED

She seems to be. I spoke to Charles.

GEORGE

He's onboard is he?

(The bell rings. Students file past. The men rise.)

TED

I believe so. I think he understood. I told him that she's too young, for one thing. Jailbait. Not the word I used though.

GEORGE

Good thing. (Momentarily gazes toward the students) Any man, any young man might be tempted, eh?

TED

I suppose so, George. I wouldn't want to be categorical. Most men, we can say that, can't we?

(George laughs.)

Still, I think there's a line that shouldn't be crossed, isn't there? Most of them are barely out of diapers.

GEORGE (more serious)

I'm completely in agreement with you there. Should anything more come up, even if seems inconsequential, immediately report it to Samuels, and to me, okay? Even if it means rocking the boat a little. There is no reason for you to take this on. We'll leave the connection to Charles out of this report, for now. Don't want to jeopardize... kids these days, eh, Ted? Anything peculiar about this "Ji"?

TED

Not that I noticed. She's involved in school theater. But her father's back in Korea. Her parents are divorced. I guess she's pretty much alone here. They all are.

GEORGE

They, Ted?

TED

These kids without fathers. The girls. They're left alone to fend for themselves.

GEORGE

Yes, it's like an epidemic. Boys, too, growing up without fathers, we shouldn't forget. But I'm wondering, what were you doing after the girl left? For that following hour or so?

TED

Working on something. A piece of writing.

GEORGE

A writer, after all. Had a notion in that direction myself some time back. Lots of people do, I guess. Well, Ted, I'm happy to have a satisfactory explanation. Still, I'll need to revise my report a bit, mention Ji, you understand, in case Dick speaks to Samuels. But for now we'll leave it out of your personnel file. You're still a young fellow. Relatively, at least, eh Ted? We don't want it to affect your future opportunities. Different spanks for different ranks, is my motto. No sign of Charles?

TED

Wonder if he dropped, after all. Maybe he's just tardy.

GEORGE

Don't forget, you have institutional support, my boy. Your job is to teach, mine to keep things running smoothly so you can do your job to the best of your abilities. I'm here to take care of anything that goes beyond normal classroom discipline and control. And you can lean on me, too, should you need someone to vent with. You understand me, I hope?

TED

Yes, I appreciate it, George. But I should go in. Don't want to miss another class.

GEORGE

Yes, we don't want that. In the future if you have to cancel, give me a heads up, okay?

TED

Will do.

GEORGE

I'll get your signature at some later date. But I'll meet with Samuels today. I'll make sure the door is open for you on time. If you have a problem getting in right now, be sure to call my cell.

TED

Okay, George. Will do.

GEORGE

Still no sign of Charles, then?

TED

He could have gone in the back way.

GEORGE

You said he's African-American, right?

TED

African, George. Came here on a student visa.

GEORGE

Lots do.

TED

Yep, more competition. Well, so long. Good talking to you.

> (The men shake hands. Ted gives a short
> wave as he exits. George takes his cell phone
> out of his pocket. Dials.)

Scene Seven

The stone steps outside the school auditorium. The doors stand open. It's windy. Ted and Ji's mother and little brother, Hung, come through the doors. Ji's mother is petite, attractive. Hung is brash, all boy. They stand in a group, smiling, waiting for Ji. Charles enters. He's inebriated. He is carrying a backpack.

TED

Charles.

CHARLES

Professor Wilson. (Pointing to mother and brother) Who's this?

YI (introducing herself)

Yi Kwan. My daughter is in the play.

CHARLES (holding up the play program)

Ji.

YI

Yes. She's "Cecily." (Laughing) Wasn't she good?

CHARLES

I couldn't keep my eyes off her.

YI

Really. Thank you.

CHARLES

I like her.

YI (confused)

You like her?

TED (glaring at Charles)

He means her performance. Translation problem.

YI (being polite)

Oh. My English not good.

CHARLES

Professor Wilson is opposed to Affirmative Action.

YI

Is he? I'm sure he has a right. What is it?

CHARLES (to Ted)

I googled it.

TED (calmly)

Good for you. (To Yi) It's not important.

CHARLES (to Yi)

Ji has a brother?

YI

Yes. This is Hung.

(Charles shakes hands with Hung.)

TED

Charles is my student.

YI

Oh. Ji is good student. She wants to go to UCLA.

(Ji enters, in street clothes. No hugs.)

I loved it, Ji. Missed identities.

JI

Mistaken...(She notices Charles. Then cooly.) Oh, Charles. ...Professor Wilson told me you were coming. I saw you in the audience.

YI

You know him?

CHARLES (to Ji)

You were bloody awesome.

JI (warming to Charles)

Thank you. Thank you for coming. Everybody. (Laughs) I sound like a Hollywood star.

YI

We could not miss it, no? But Hung says he doesn't want to come tomorrow night. He says he doesn't understand adult comedy.

JI

Took me a long time.

(Everyone smiles, awkwardly)

CHARLES (abruptly, to Ted)

I'm not supposed to be here now, right man? According to our contract.

TED

It's a free country, ultimately.

(Charles slings his backpack from one shoulder to the other.)

CHARLES

Free to starve, you mean.

TED (quietly)

No job yet?

CHARLES (starkly)

No.

TED

Sorry to hear that.

YI

Not always land of plenty. But we keep trying.

CHARLES (aggressive again)

But I'm not supposed to work at all. (To Yi) No green card. I'm not entitled.

HUNG (protective)

My mother understands, Charles.

TED

Yes, enough, Charles. This is not your night, is it?

CHARLES

You're right, man, I came to see Ji. I've got front row tomorrow again, too. (to Ji, more graciously). You were awesome. The star of Act II. I liked where you pick up books and throw them on the table. Where she says those three horrids.

JI (in character)

"Horrid Political Economy! Horrid Geography! Horrid, horrid German!"

CHARLES (laughing)

And it's only studying them that she finds horrid!

TED

Right!

                         JI
I hate to study, too!

                         YI
Ji, in front of professor!

                         JI
I like to act!

                         CHARLES
Yes, and it requires an audience to make it real.

                         JI
Yes!

                         CHARLES (cheered)
I'll take my leave, now.

                         JI
Your what?

                         CHARLES
I must go, Ji.

                         (He folds up his play program and puts it in
                         his back pocket. Waving his hand gallantly,
                         and drunkenly, he exits.)

                         TED (almost proud)
I told you he was smart.

                         (A blank response from the others to this.)

JI

But I don't like that he calls you "man" like he own you.

TED (trying to keep lightened mood, turning to Yi)

Local slang, I guess. In Africa.

YI

Very rude, I think. Was he drinking? I thought I smell.

TED

I think maybe, yes.

YI (skeptical)

He comes twice? (To Ji) He likes you? (To Ted) No boyfriend until she graduates.

TED (mollifying)

Charles? He likes plays.

YI

He's black.

JI

Oh, my God, Mom!

HUNG (pointing off-stage)

Like Principal Samuels.

TED

Oh, that's him.

(We see Samuels talking to a female student. He looks like a former football player.

His head is cocked to try to catch what the
student is saying. He glances at Ted and the
group.)

JI

How do you know him, Hung? (Concerned) He's looking at us.

HUNG

Don't you remember I came to your freshman orientation? Samuels gave a long
speech.

JI (nervously looking over at Samuels as she
speaks)

Hung is too smart for his own good. Plays four instruments. Show off.

HUNG

Two of them are almost the same.

TED

But you play them differently?

JI (turning back to group)

See, Mom. Funny like in the play.

YI

I see and hear perfectly, Ji. Sorry about the boy, I just meant very black. Almost
blue. (Laughing) I'm almost orange.

TED

Me, almost transparent.

JI

We make you fat. Mom is a good cook.

YI

Ji! (Then) But maybe we invite professor for dinner sometime, yes.

TED

Thank you, I'd love that. I don't cook myself. Only microwaves. Mostly macaroni and cheese.

YI (teasingly to Ted)

Ji can barely do noodles.

JI

I can boil an egg.

(Laughter. Pause.)

TED

I must go, too, I'm afraid. Much enjoyed the play, Ji. You were terrific.

JI

Thank you, Ted.

YI

Ji!

JI

Thank you, professor.

(Ted shakes hands with all three. Hung starts to walk away.)

YI

Hung, say goodbye!

(Hung walks back a few paces. The four appear as if a family tableau.)

187

                              TED (to Ji)

See you tomorrow night.

                              YI

You come again? I'll leave Hung with aunt. He won't be sad.

                              TED

Okay, thanks, I enjoy the company. (To Ji) Don't worry.

                              JI

Okay, not worry.

                              YI

What worry? Worry what, "Ji"?

                              TED (covering)

About the performance, right?

                              JI

Yeah. If first performance went all right, second time likely bad. It is easy to fail.

                              YI

Oh, okay.

                              JI (diverting)

Can I drive?

                              HUNG

I'll walk.

                              YI (to Ted)

She just got licence.

TED

Really? Happy Birthday.

JI

Thank you.

YI (to Ted)

How you know it is birthday?

JI

Mom, everybody here gets licence on sixteenth birthday.

YI

Oh, okay. See you tomorrow, professor.

TED

Ted, please.

YI

Yi. But you know already.

TED

Yi and Ji. Whose idea was that?

YI

Her father's.

HUNG

Bye, Ted.

YI and JI

Hung!

(Ted exits. The other three stand there for a moment, the family tableau broken.)

Scene Eight

On the steps outside of the auditorium, before the play is to begin. Still windy. Three or four people, including Ted, mill around waiting for the doors to open. Ted wears jeans but has donned a sport coat for the occasion. He stealthily pulls a flask from his coat and drinks. He puts the flask back inside his coat. He sits down on the steps. Yi arrives. She is carrying a small plastic tupperware.

TED (rising)

Yi.

YI

I brought dessert. And roses for Ji. Hung says it is tradition. (Holding up tupperware) Korean treat.

TED

How nice of you. No Hung tonight?

YI

He is coming later with cousin. Ji was mad he didn't want to come.

TED

Cousin? So Ji is not so alone.

YI

Boy cousin, her age. She doesn't like. She says he is too immature. We are early, yes?

TED

A bit. I love Korean barbeque. Not kimchi, though, I'm afraid. (He laughs.) But I've never had Korean dessert. Or don't remember doing so.

YI

Old family recipe.

(She laughs. Lowers head. He takes off his sport coat, folds it, and puts it on a step.)

YI

Oh, not necessary.

TED

Sit, please. Old family coat.

(She sits.)

YI (rising, laughing)

Something hard in coat.

TED

Oh, stupid of me.

(He readjusts coat so the flask is in a different spot.)

A book.

(She smiles, sits again. He sits down beside her.)

YI

What are you? May I ask?

TED

Me? You mean, heritage. WASP. White Anglo-Saxon Protestant, the original settlers. My family traces its ancestry back to the...not that I care much. But "blood is thicker than water" my mother always said. When I was a kid I didn't know what that meant. "Tougher where there isn't any," was another saying of hers I didn't understand, at first.

191

YI

I don't think I understand.

TED

Sorry. I mean...maybe I can explain another time.

YI

Yes. I'm interested in families. I like to learn. America is complicated place. Korea simple. Very organized.

(She opens the tupperware.)

You try?

TED

I'd love to.

(He takes a piece. Bites.)

Oh, delicious. Sweet and sour.

YI

Thank you. I'm glad you like.

TED

I do.

YI

I'm glad.

(Ted feels his pants pocket and pulls out a cell phone.)

TED

Sorry. I think I should read this. Urgent, it says. From the college. I get texts, but I've never sent one myself. To anyone.

YI

No problem.

TED (rising)

One second.

YI (rising)

I just take roses to Ji. Backstage.

TED

Oh, usually it's after...yes, do. I'm sure she'll be pleased. They're beautiful.

> (Yi exits left. Ted moves center stage right. Lights dim on theater building and steps. He squints at the phone.)

Not George? Kathy Osborn? Who is Kathy Osborn? What is a Professional Development Coordinator? If this is about climbing over the walls...(he reads aloud) "Professor James, I'm sorry to inform you that due to failure to fulfill your flex obligation–my what?–$200 will be extracted from your upcoming pay-check. This is the second year of the flex program and derelict faculty are being held accountable this year."

> (Ted turns his back, looks around, reaches his coat for flask but then thinks better of it. He sits down next to his coat, his head between his knees, and continues reading aloud.)

TED

"I wanted to give you a heads up. I've sent many emails, but have never heard…"

(George enters, and stands over him.)

GEORGE

Ted.

TED (looks up, surprised)

George.

(He slips the cell phone into his front pocket.)

GEORGE (blithely, yet eyeing Ted)

Samuels invited me. Said it was a strong production. The best they'd done…since *The Crucible*, I think he said. Don't know that play myself.

(Ted stands. He carefully puts on his coat.)

TED

About the Salem witch trials.

GEORGE

Oh, of course, I remember it now. You were here last night, too, Ted? Samuels said he saw you.

TED

Did he? Surprised he knew who I was. How did he? I don't know him, since he's apparently never around except for plays.

GEORGE

He would be expected to attend the play as he's the principal of the school. He must have seen you in the office, Ted. You seem a bit edgy, my boy. Is something wrong? I interrupted something?

TED

No. No. (Then) Do you know a Kathy Osborn?

GEORGE

Professional Development? Only by name.

TED

What a joke. I put their kids through college—probably private school—I make their fulsome salaries possible by working at slave wages and now she's telling me that their "extracting" money from *my* paycheck. She says "extracting" not "deducting." Can you believe this...well, never mind. Something about a flex obligation.

GEORGE

That's where you're expected to attend some seminar or conference or something. If there's anything I can do to help?

TED

No, but thanks. It really takes the cake, that's all.

GEORGE

Speaking of, I didn't mean to interrupt your supper, Ted.

TED

No, no, just dessert.

(He reaches down and picks up the tupperware container.)

TED

Would you like some? It's...homemade!

GEORGE

Is it? Thank you, I will. Not much fresh since the wife died. You cook, Ted?

TED

Not this. From a friend. She...

GEORGE

She, you say?

TED (brusquely)

Yes.

(He closes container, looks round toward where Yi exited.)

If I may, George, how did you come to discuss me with Samuels?

GEORGE

It just came up casually, in reference to the report. Your problem student—and Ji, is it? But, as promised, I didn't connect your staying late to Charles. Samuels said she was a bit of problem student herself.

TED

What, Ji? How could she be? I mean, she's in the play tonight.

GEORGE

I know.

TED

She offered me a ticket for tonight and I felt I couldn't really say no. Besides, I liked the play so much I decided to come again. It *is* a fine production. I'll have to give Steiglitz that. He's the drama teacher. When I wrote–you know, long time ago–it was drama. So you see my interest is fully accounted for. And she...

GEORGE (eyes Ted further)

I didn't say it wasn't... accounted for, as you say. I'm just here to see the play myself. Nothing more.

TED

But what do you mean by "problem student"?

GEORGE

There was an issue with one of the male teachers, according to Samuels.

TED

Impossible! She's barely sixteen.

GEORGE

Well, kids grow up fast these days, I'm sure you've noticed. And it wouldn't be the first time, would it, that some student had a crush on a teacher?

TED

She's Korean!

GEORGE

I'll tell you something, Ted, about Ji–but this is just between us, okay? Don't want more trouble than we already have...

TED

What trouble?

GEORGE

Hold on. Don't get defensive. Samuels told me this girl Ji would occasionally stop him in the hallways and even once or twice came by his office after classes. She'd make excuses. He thought it was odd. He told her to get involved in a school activity. She was new on campus, apparently. Lonely. New to America. Well, I guess she took his advice.

TED (more controlled, yet still on edge)

That's what he calls a problem student? Maybe he's the male teacher. Why would you believe him anyway?

(At that moment gunshots are heard. Ji comes running out of the auditorium. She's wearing her Cicely costume, circa 1890's.)

JI (screaming)

He's shot. He had a gun. I saw it.

(She throws herself into Ted's arms and buries her head in his breast. George goes into combat mode, from his pockets drawing a gun in one hand and cell phone in the other.)

GEORGE (on phone)

There's been a shooting. Cleveland High School. Yes, South Street. Hurry. A man's been shot.

(Ted lifts Ji's chin.)

TED

Shot? Who Ji? (He grabs her) Charles?

JI (whimpering)

Principal Samuels. Charles shot him.

TED

Charles?

JI

The Principal. Right in the face. There was a river of blood flowing down his face. I think he's dead.

GEORGE

You're not sure, young lady?

JI

He looked dead. It was like a red river on the floor. Almost black. Pooling underneath the seats. He had dead look.

GEORGE

I'll call security. Dick. (to Ji) Where's Charles?

(On a back screen we see a silhouette of Charles with a gun in his hand. Ji, in semi-shock, appears not to hear George. Then...)

JI

He ran. He ran backstage. And then out into the parking lot, I think. Where is my mother? He still had the gun in his hand.

TED

You're mother went backstage to see you.

JI

Oh my god.

TED (to George)

You always carry?

JI

I've got to find uh ma.

GEORGE

It didn't have to come to this, Ted. My God. (Then professional again) You stay with her. Get her out of sight. Don't leave her. Not for a second. I'll find your mother, Ji.

(Sirens are heard. Ted and Ji quickly exit. Blackout. Immediately we see them in a spotlight under the tree. She stands behind him, her arms wrapped around his waist. We don't see her face.)

JI

I didn't do anything. I didn't do anything.

TED (not looking at her, on guard)

Of course you didn't.

JI

I feel shame.

(He turns and faces her.)

TED

Did you see everything?

JI

Principal Samuels went up to Charles and asked him what he was doing there. I don't know how Charles got in. He was sitting alone in the auditorium. He was calling out my name. "Ji!" Ji!" Like a simply ugly chant. "Ji!" It echoed throughout the theater. I could hear it backstage. I was getting my make-up on. "Ji," he screamed. I walk out on the proscenium. And that's when Principal came in.

    (Spotlight switches to the back, where we see Principal Samuels and Charles.)

SAMUELS

What are you doing here, son?

CHARLES (yelling)

None of your bloody business.

SAMUELS (cupping his ear)

What did you say?

    (Principal Samuels starts toward him and Charles shoots. There are streams of red flowing down Principal's face. Spotlight switches back to Ted and Ji.)

JI

It was horrible. I only went to Principal Samuels for school help.

TED

What? What are you saying?

    (More sirens. Flashing red lights fill the stage.)

The police are here. Don't worry.

JI

I hope Hung didn't come.

TED

We'll find them when everything clears. Are you saying Charles might have a reason to take things out on Samuels?

(Ji buries her head in Ted's chest. Then looks up.)

JI

I didn't do anything with Principal Samuels! Just like nothing with Charles. Nor anybody else. Nothing! And Stieglitz is gay! People said things, but it was only gossip.

TED

Okay. Okay. I believe you. There's no way Charles would know even if you had— would he? ...Could he?

JI

People are just mean. There was nothing. Nada. Gossip. Charles talked to my friend, Lya. You remember her? I don't know what she told him. But it's all gossip. Just like between us. And we haven't done anything.

(He lets go of her.)

TED

Who said something about us? God, I'll never work again in this town.

JI

Samuels. To Stieglitz. Yesterday.

TED

Stieglitz again!

JI

Mr. Stieglitz said people talk. He said I shouldn't listen. Block it out. He said I was wonderful last night.

TED (looking toward the theater building)
You were, yes. But...

JI
Now it will be the only night. Probably never again in a school play! (Holding on
to him again) Oh, Ted, I feel so much sorry. I only want my mom. Charles is crazy.

TED (abstractly)
I liked him, saw myself in him, I guess. He realized that one's own mind is a tor-
ture chamber—that you don't have to look elsewhere. (More focused) But I never
thought it would come to this. Ji, you can't say anything to anybody. Nothing on
background. Just the killing itself. Just describe what you saw, just...

(Dick enters.)

DICK
I thought maybe I'd find you two here.

(Ji releases Ted)

TED
What's happened? Is Samuels dead? Did they catch Charles?

(A pause. He looks skeptically at the two of them.)

DICK
The black boy? He's on the loose. Still on the grounds somewhere, I expect. Only one
gate is open. Principal Samuels, no, I think he'll survive. His face was half shot off
though. I thought I'd seen it all in Afghanistan. I wish I had a gun myself right now.

TED (suddenly)
Stay here with her. Don't leave her.

(He starts to go.)

DICK

No, sir, you can't do that. I've got my job to do.

(Ted is about to run off.)

JI

Ted!

DICK

You call him "Ted"?

(Ted turns around toward them.)

TED

I've got to find him. And your mother.

(Ted starts to run off. The flask falls from his coat pocket and smashes loudly on the ground. Ted stops, tears off his sport coat. Exits. The spotlight shifts from the tree to a high chainlink fence. Charles is half way up attempting to climb over it. He wears a red jacket which contrasts with the black and white quality of the lighting.)

Charles!

(Charles turns to look at Ted and flashes the gun.)

CHARLES

Stay away, professor. ...Is he dead?

TED

Samuels? He'll survive, they say—and so can you, Charles.

(Charles drops to the ground.)

CHARLES (near tears)

Why didn't you bloody help me?

TED

I don't know what you mean, Charles. With Ji? She's not into you. Or you forced it too much, too fast, maybe. Buy why Samuels, I want to know?

CHARLES

Why? Because she played with him, too. You're not so special, you know, professor, when it comes to Ji...or anything. You're just another writer want-to-be. Don't you know that. Don't you know I saw that right away. Your sad drinking and lust for Ji and acceptance of faggots and Hemingway nihilism. Your talk of your disappointments, all that bloody inward shit.

(Charles toys with the gun.)

I bet you've never shot a gun, huh professor? I'm right, right? Never seen anyone really hurt. Never seen fingers cut off with a machete. Never been anywhere, really. Never seen children with AIDS dying alone or maybe raised by a sister because they parents have already died.

TED (unflinchingly)

I'm supposed to feel guilty about belonging to a civilized society. Or one that used to be, at least—before everybody had a gun. And before people like you...

CHARLES (holding out the gun)

Careful.

TED (his muster up—but sort of mechanically)
Before the flood gates were opened, crowding the schools, reducing much of it to remediation. I'm not mourning my own losses, Charles, as much as I'm mourning the loss of America.

CHARLES

I don't know what's more pathetic, your racism or your nostalgia. Maybe they're the same thing. But you made an exception for Ji, huh, Professor James?

TED

I suppose that's true. And for you as well. But otherness is hardwired, we know that much. We build each other's ghetto, as it were. And people like their own better than someone else's, thinking at least they own it. You're the one who shot Samuels, Charles, shot a black man, not me. You're right, I don't own a gun. Never have. Never will. But I still don't understand why him?

CHARLES

He got in the bloody way. That's enough, isn't it?

TED

In the way of what? But don't be stupid, Charles. They'll catch you sooner or later.

(George enters, gun out, aims it at Charles.)

GEORGE

Drop the gun, son!

CHARLES (looking off in the distance)
You're lucky I respect you, professor. Respect your learning.

(He raises the gun to his head. George fires just as Charles fires.)

206

(Lights down and quickly back up. Ted, George, Dick, Ji, and Yi stand in a circle around the dead body of Charles. Ji is shaking, wrapped in her mother's arms. Yi still holds the dark red roses which match the pool of blood next to Charles.)

YI

I'm glad Hung didn't see this.

GEORGE (to Dick)

Where the fuck are the police?

DICK

I guess they haven't found the entrance. The place is otherwise locked. I came when I heard the shots. What happened?

(A moment of silence.)

TED (looking at George)

It was...suicide. (Then half to himself) You wonder if he ever had a chance.

(Ji takes the roses from her mother and places them beside Charles.)

(Two policeman arrive on scene.)

Dick (to the cops)

You're too late, I'm afraid.

BLACKOUT

END OF PLAY

Tyrannos

A Play In Two Acts

"No law, no divinity: Gold, force and Venus rule."

Egidio of Viterbo

Characters

President Richard Cadmus, sixties, white
Basia, his third wife and (possibly) half-sister, early thirties
Richie, twelve, son from his third wife
Speaker of the House Jim Meadows, fifties, white
Stuart Adams, presidential aide, twenties
Protestor, a college-age male
Olivia, a Homeland Security aide, twenties
Jack, a Secret Service agent
A second Secret Service agent
Server One, black, a middle-aged man
Server Two, black, a young man
New York mayoral candidate
Army Soldier
Crowd

Act I takes place July 3 at an International Hotel in New York City and Act II
July 4 and a few days after at the White House.

Act One

Scene One

A campaign-style dinner and rally in a large ballroom reminiscent of a Greek or Roman temple. The principal characters sit at a dais, eating dinner. The two servers, dressed in red jackets, stand stage right near a cart that contains pitchers of water and bottles of wine, both white and red. A TV camera is to the house front right of the stage. A microphone is in the center of the dais. President Cadmus stands at the microphone. He is wearing a blue suit with a red tie. He is a bit overweight, but still handsome. His blond hair is long-ish, blow-dried, looks almost coiffed.

He is a former business tycoon, but he is on a level above the cynical business type—is delusional, self-convinced but at the same time has an eye for grandeur, and a certain, misguided heroism. The gathered stop eating and look toward the President as he begins his remarks.

CADMUS (enjoying himself)

Oh children of America, born and bred here the same, there is a reason why we draw the largest, and tonight I must say best-dressed, crowds...

(Laughter from the audience)

...why you gather here in this great hotel, in—may I say this, this beautiful hotel I built—may I say that?—why you, unlike my boring, defeated opponent who never could raise such a crowd, scarcely a quorum, in support of her failed, unexciting campaign last fall—no one thought I could win, right? No one thought I could solve the riddle of the populace. Well, I did, and now it's time to make America great again, take back our country from those who have aligned themselves with their own interests and not the interests of the hard-working people of our country—though I am not sure you guys are so hard-working...

(Again, genial laughter)

But I know you are patriots. They looks down on us, those of us who make their living on trade. Tonight, we gather to raise money for a man I need to fight the fight with me, the next great mayor of New York! (He nods charmingly toward a man to his right on the dais, but then returns to his own story.) I'm always happy to be back here on home ground, home ground which before becoming President I kept buying up! Tonight we raise money—lots of money, I know you guys have it. Tomorrow we celebrate July 4th. Our great independence. But we all know neither New York nor the rest of the country is as beautiful as once it was. You, I know, have come here suppliant—but as proud Americans, proud of our country, or soon to be again—asking for my help. I am the only one who can fix it. Our previous leaders lacked the courage, the smarts, foresight really, the will, to deal with this scourge, this plague of illegals that has swamped our beloved nation—this infestation—the worst elements allowed in, bringing in crime, bringing in drugs, rapists... without a strong border, you don't really have a country, do you?

CROWD

No!

CADMUS

Without a strong border, wages are driven lower, refugees get better healthcare than our own citizens. Will we let our country be overrun?

CROWD

No!

CADMUS

Our enemies claim I'm racist. I have a Jewish grandchild for God's sakes. This isn't about racial purity. It's about nationalism.

CROWD

Right on! Hurrah!

(Cadmus bathes in the adoration, waits for
the crowd to settle.)

SERVER TWO (quietly to Servant One)

Here we go again. This train is pulling into the same station.

SERVER ONE

Remember, the President doesn't drink.

SERVER TWO

He should.

CADMUS (less charmingly)

Tomorrow, in Washington, in honor of our great country on its birthday, I
will announce a new initiative to take back our beautiful country. And those
who profit most from bringing illegals in–are you all listening?–those coy-
otes who take the last savings of those who head out on the road with their
families, will pay the dearest price, believe me. My predecessor tried to hand-
pick his successor, but the people demanded change. An end to America as
patsy–all the while the piggy bank–to the world. Was he, my predecessor,
even legitimate–can I ask that? Was he born in America? I mean his father
was African. Do you think his birth certificate is genuine? I don't know.
I don't know. We will never know. But we know he was a disaster for our
country. That he opened the floodgates to every Tom, Dick, or Harry–rather
every Diego, Abdul...

(Subdued, uncomfortable laughter. Cadmus
realizes he's gone off script. Goes to sip
his water but finds it empty. Servant One,
glowering at Servant Two, rushes to fill it.

(An awkward pause. Cadmus gestures to the
walls.)

Look at those tall mirrors, will you? Look at that marble. (Smiling good-
naturedly at Servant One) Flows like water. Breccia Pernice, they call it, a
very rare marble—a blend of rose, peach, and pink, that took our breath away
when we first saw it. I looked at a bunch of marbles. But wasn't satisfied
until I saw this one. Of course it was incredibly expensive. No expense was
spared, including hiring the best marble cutters, the finest craftsman. I've
got great admiration for craftsman like that, whatever the cost. And yet we
always came in under budget, and on time. My father taught me, time is money. Spend it wisely! But time has almost run out for our great nation. We have
to be tough, very very tough, and we have to be smart. Relentless. Secure
the border! Build the wall! Big beautiful prisons, too. I know how to build
things, believe me. Look around you, this great hotel in a prime location. I
went to the best colleges, you know. I graduated from the Sloan School of
Business. My uncle was a professor at Princeton. We always admired Uncle
Steve. But let me be perfectly clear, I was accepted on my own merit! ...To
tell you the truth, though, I couldn't wait to get out of school. I wanted to
go to work. I've worked very, very hard. Not like some of you hedge fund
managers I see here.

(Quiet laughter)

(Stuart, sitting far stage left at the dais, turns
and whispers into the ear of Speaker of the
House Meadows to his left. Stuart is dressed
stylishly—like Cadmus— while Meadows more
plainly. In perhaps a plain dark blue suit.)

I don't drink. But I love the look of glasses of red and white wine on a beautiful banquet table! Notice the blue table cloth! I like details. Things in order.
My wife, our great First Lady, Basia, makes fun of me cause walking down the

Presidential portrait gallery I'll stop to straighten a picture. There's one or two I don't straighten though!

> (Laughter. Cadmus strokes his hair. Sips the water.)

> STUART (setting down his glass of white wine, with a slight Texas accent, amused, conspiratorially)

I love listening to our President, don't you, Mr. Speaker? Maybe he doesn't read much, but he knows how to read a room. He doesn't think like readers think—he's moved beyond that, links, and distracts. We've escaped from his predecessor's lame piety and melancholy. Go all out, squander, I say. He's acting, having fun. Saying the kinds of things in the playscript of our imaginations. Boy-Howdy, we're all having fun again—our kind of fun. I have a friend just like Cadmus, feels the responsibility to be entertaining, make the party more fun.

> (Meadows sips his glass of red wine.)

> MEADOWS

I'd say you do your part, too, Stuart.

> STUART

Thank you, I try!

> MEADOWS

I did grow tired of speeches full of parallel structure—I swear the last president thought he was a minister. I go to church for that.

> (Stuart laughs. Meadows drinks again.)

MEADOWS

But Cadmus is the president now. I'm not sure he really understands what that means. Where he's landed. Falsely believing, in my view, that if he creates an alternative reality he'll be untouchable.

STUART

It's all part of the fun. Who would have ever expected a President to act in such a manner. Of course we know that in private presidents are not so stiff. In Cadmus' case, the private id is displayed in public. And what an id it is. As if to say, you need only yourself, it's enough.

CADMUS (ready again)

I've taken tremendous risks, you know that, don't you? But they've paid off. I have a beautiful life. A beautiful wife–home this evening with our young son– not to mention all my beautiful adult children. I'm rich–I'm very, very rich–but now I want to do something not for myself but for this nation I love. No one is sicker than am I about what has happened to our beautiful country, believe me. We will reclaim our homeland. Our country will not become a migrant camp, a refugee holding-center, trust me.

>(Cheers, standing ovation. He again touches his hair.)

>STUART (drinking wine; his delivery is almost choral, but only Meadows hears him. At times he stops and breathes through his nose. Uses hand gestures. He shakes his head in amazement.)

The Old Gods return. Return, raise their heads, find their celebrant, wouldn't you say so, Jim? Titans of industry, not merely government or the military. Surely you agree we need a man who can, as he said, enjoy himself, who goes to the golf links–I once played with him–like a king to the hunt, hounds yelping. Puts Hamlet to the test. It's Barnum and Bailey that cheers us best. Promoters, not existentialists. True, at one time he was a robber baron–but as a professor of mine at Yale once said, of Peer Gynt, "Ultimately he's too vitalistic and metaphoric to abide in any role, his self-absorption produces pragmatic disinterestedness." He'll look after your farmers, Jim, that you can be sure of. In times when mores are influx, self-fashioning pushes us forward. (More quietly) It's even okay to be white again, and ironically, not even Christian–but forgive me, I know you are a believer, Mr. Speaker. And that you served.

MEADOWS

I am. I did.

STUART

But it's something, isn't it, this reassertion of pure being–the trail of heterogeneity, and even Darwin, flattened by will, and freedom. Myself, I'm on board. It's thrilling, really. The alpha male, equipped–she, his opponent, wasn't gypped–is augur to his own birds, putting America first. The end of diversity, difference, at last, we ourselves sufficient, sir. This suits me this rhetoric of naturalism, of the Natural Man, personal freedom, idiosyncracy.

CADMUS

Thank you. Thank you. Now sit and enjoy yourselves. Enjoy this beautiful environment. People should enjoy their lives. That chandelier, it cost a fortune. It's sad, people going about just enjoying their lives and then there's a crime, there's crime. It doesn't have to happen. It didn't need to come to this point. My predecessors let it happen. But we are going to put a stop to it.

> (Some commotion as everyone, including Cadmus, sits again. He turns to speak to the mayoral candidate. There's a clattering of forks as everyone, but Stuart, digs in.)

STUART

His love of conflict, the sea-driven bitching, even the self-pity, grievances, the mix, I'm persuaded by it.

MEADOWS

In order to justify your own indulgences?

(Stuart toasts, laughs, acknowledging the jibe.)

If you're asking if I like, in my half century or so, becoming a minority, I don't. Or treated as a criminal just for acting like a man—I mean, when did we become the bad guys? I've worked all my life. I also understand the workings of government. A great leader practices detachment, Stuart. (Exasperated, voice rising) Democracy requires patience, resolve. His predecessor had that at least. I fear this man wants little more than to destroy his predecessor's legacy. All this pageantry, military parades, bombast is an attempt to drive away doubts of legitimacy.

STUART

It's simply a more vigorous version of patriotism, that's all it is. Surely American pageantry starting to pall is a death knell.

MEADOWS

It's legislation that The House of Representatives must produce not pageantry— or trust me I will not be Speaker long. The other party will flip the House this November. *That* is what I fear. The President is disdainful of all but dictatorial leaders, CEO's.

STUART

Alliances shift—what worked for years may not work well now, may no longer serve our interests.

MEADOWS

I'm from the Midwest...your word means something there. We don't rail or strut like those out of Queens, or must I say it, Texans like you, Stuart! No, I shan't be convinced—you won't convince me—his temperament is a liability, however right I am with the policies.

(Meadows looks around, then quietly)

Let's move over here. That camera catches most everything.

> (The two men grab their glasses of wine, and stand house front left. They pace around, and at times crossing in opposite directions, as they continue. It appears slightly absurd.)

I tell you it's the insults, Stuart. He spares not even our war heroes? It's totally unnecessary, really beyond the pale–not to mention, yes, unChristian. And the bragging?

STUART

He's in the tradition of the self-praising Greeks. Or Whitman.

> MEADOWS (non-responsive, half to himself)

I have no kids, but if I did I don't think I could go home and say this man is what America stands for. Not after all the insults, the falsehoods.

STUART

It's not really lying, it's a counter-narrative. Postmodern. Or as Michelson wrote of deSade: "Of a self-consciously fluid juxtaposition of rhetorical and real arguments: If not all of them please, surely a few will!"

> MEADOWS (further exasperated)

Bullcocky, postmodern, don't quote postmodern to me...and all the young women? All of them blond, too. Like Langford's new aide in Homeland. What's her name?

STUART

Olivia. It was Langford who approved her.

MEADOWS

Oh, he did, did he.

STUART (laughingly)

Do I detect a bit of envy?

MEADOWS (defensively)

You do not.

STUART

The women are the fruits of his labor. His love of beauty no doubt a reminder of his youth–I don't kid myself. He's OCD, narcissistic. But everyone needs something, for the President it's women. Some gamble, some watch old movies. Others turn to porn. (Then directly toward Meadows) Some alcohol, right? (Again rhetorical) You aren't going to keep someone from something they need. People don't change–(half to himself) even if they at times can redistribute. No dude changed his times more, while insulting so many, as did Martin Luther, whom you no doubt admire.

MEADOWS (incensed)

Luther? He was a true religious man! This man is thrice married!

(Cadmus engaged with others up to then, takes notice of the heated conversation between Stuart and Meadows.)

STUART

Luther argued in favor of divorce. (leaning forward, more measured, again intimate, conspiratorial) Give the man a chance. Less than two years on the job. We need to counter these strong men and reactionaries we see around the world with a strong-man of our own–American-made. Product of the best schools, best economy. But a populist. A patrician nativist, if you will–the complete man among partial men. (Mildly defensive) If he insults too readily, it is only in the absence of an honest debate. He'll treat you well if you treat him the same. (Then pointed) Still, everyone is on notice, I agree, he'll brook no disloyalty. (More directly at Meadows) Surely, you too are on his side, Mr. Speaker? Am I right?

MEADOWS (half-kiddingly)

I shan't take that as a threat, Stuart.

(Stuart drinks. Scans the scene, the building. Nods to the President, who turns back to chat with the mayoral candidate.)

STUART

Who would I be to threaten the Speaker of the House?

(Servant Two, now pouring wine, carrying a tray, walks over to the two men.)

SERVER TWO

More wine, sirs.

STUART

I'm fine, thank you.

(Meadows holds out his glass. The servant pours.)

MEADOWS

Thank you, young man. Nectar of the gods.

(Server Two retreats, moves among those on the dais.)

STUART (resuming)

I choose the Overman, Mr. Speaker, choose a man not driven to worlds other than this. (Half to himself) Your alter ego going rogue is not the worst thing that can happen. (Again raises his glass) I drink to him who won't be handled. Progressives fail to understand that their liberalism, globalism, if you will, is so damned provincial—that the rest of us care about ourselves and our own community first, this place and this history and heritage determining—I read this somewhere—its own character for itself, deciding who is and who is not a citizen. Say I, let Cadmus be Cadmus!

> (Meadows manages a smile, but shakes his head appalled at the same time. He sets down his fork. Drinks.)

MEADOWS

I have to wonder what's in it for you, Stuart.

STUART

Besides the sheer poetry of it?

MEADOWS

There's the poetry of plain truth, too, you know.

> (A young protestor carrying a sign reading "Stop Separating Families! appears directly to the right of Stuart.)

CROWD

How did he get in! Grab him!

> (Two Secret Service agents are immediately upon him, taking him down. They bring him to his feet, pat him down.)

CADMUS (standing up)

No, let him speak! I'm not afraid of anything he might say. I've no reason to be. I've done nothing wrong. Have nothing to hide.

(The Secret Service let go of his arms, remain standing next to him.)

PROTESTOR (sarcastic)

Nothing to hide, you say? Release your income taxes then, let us see how you acquired such great wealth. Colluding with foreign powers was it, Mr. President?

CADMUS

Foreign powers? What nonsense–I got my money from my father...(realizing his admission)...a loan paid back with interest when I made my millions.

PROTESTOR

No foreign influence? Then explain how was it your wife, your sister, got into the country, Mr. President?

CADMUS

My sister, what has she to do with anything?

PROTESTOR

I mean, the model. Oh, how stupid of me to forget, all your wives were models. All three–and your sister, whom you are married to.

CADMUS (to the crowd)

More nonsense? My sister is a respected doctor, a brilliant person, with a family of her own. (To the protestor) How can I argue with someone as incoherent as you. (To the Secret Service) Throw him out, after all. Send him home to daddy.

CROWD

Let's us take care of him. Deport him! Vermin!

CADMUS (smiling, egging them on)

If I weren't President, I'd punch him right in the face.

CROWD

We will take care of him!

> (The Protestor, again held by the Secret Service, is about to be removed.)

> PROTESTOR (turning back his head to yell)

I say nonetheless, yes, your sister is your wife.

> CADMUS (half to himself)

Still on my sister are you? My sister? (Motions for them to release him again. Regains his poise.) No more than you are my equal. How could she be my sister, may I ask, she's an immigrant! And she's young enough...

> (Cadmus doesn't want to go there.)

> PROTESTOR

Yes, very young. Of whom you fail yet to say, again, how came she here. My country, too, I must add.

> CADMUS

Basia is my wife! She is a great lady. The First Lady. (Aside–bewildered) I had a terrible dream last night though, about her being my mother.

> PROTESTOR

But legally, who let her in? There's a special exemption for beautiful models is there?

> CADMUS (wobbled, but counterpunching)

At least you recognize beauty. Take a look around you, look at this great hotel I built! You are the one conspiring, conspiring with the national media, to make wild accusations, to thwart the will of the people. You and your like are the enemy of the people. Never will you people accept the fact that you lost the election. Lost it fair and square. But I remain unfazed, I know how to go around such as you...

PROTESTOR (sarcastic)

You know so little. Things to come to light will blindside you. You will understand more than you do now about family values that your party claims to cherish! The sins of the father—your father—will be clear to all. Where is your wife's *real* birth certificate? What goes around comes around, Mr. President. Your deflecting and changing the subject will not suffice then.

CADMUS (speaking more generally to the assembled)

Deflect? Change the subject? (Points to his head) Rather I use my head. I have a very high I.Q., believe me—and go directly to the people. Believe me, we will start over again—(pointing at protestor) your day is over. We'll take action. Deport people who illegally enter our beautiful country, bringing their children with them, using their children in such an awful manner, we will send them back without a trial! Put an end to asylum seekers once and for all!

PROTESTOR

And separate families at the border! Separate children from their mothers! Have you no shame, sir?

CADMUS (further shaken)

Who says we do that? But we would have every right. They are not our citizens and do not enjoy the privileges given to our citizens. (Turns to crowd) Am I right?

CROWD

Yes!

CADMUS

Unlike my predecessor—I will never speak his name—I am a man of action. Yes, I make deals, but only from a position of strength, once again the world will respect us. No one thought I could win the election, no...but I, Cadmus, did so.

> (He can tell that the routine sounds a bit
> hollow, but regains his stride. Addresses the
> protestor directly again.)

Go home to daddy, crying to mommy. It's way past your bedtime, I think. Or better, get a job.

Support your family. Play by the rules. Be a man. There was a time in our country when loyal men—and loyal women, too—respected the flag, respected our country. Now you have highly paid athletes taking a knee at professional soccer games during our national anthem to protest what they call racial injustice. All the while someone in the national media is going to say glibly that soldiers died so that those pro players have the freedom to take a knee!

> PROTESTOR (undeterred, but fanatically)

They say you killed your brother. Drove him to his death. Cut him out of the family will. Cut off benefits to his children. You yourself are the plague we suffer, are the pollution that soils everything and coarsens discourse, you and those sycophants who sit there beside you, eating their five-course meals. A red wave is coming, but it's not for your party! I thank you for tearing the cover off the cesspool that is your followers. We will put a stop to the pollution of greed and intolerance, killers and stoics who can't accept that they no longer live in gated communities. It's we who will act, and stop the tearing of little children, babies, from their mother's, and father's, arms. (Driving in the stake) Perhaps your brother Andy would have understood! Perhaps he knew too much!

> CADMUS

I've heard enough!

> (But then, as if a ghost has been summoned)

How dare you speak of my brother. Who are you to use his name. Who. (Half to himself) Yes, it's true, he had a very difficult life, very, very difficult, a life crippled by alcohol. It was very, very sad. But I had nothing but love for my brother. He had a very tough life, very tough. He was a terrific guy, and plenty smart–but didn't get the Queens street-fighting gene (Turns to the crowd) One time I said to him, even though he was five years my senior–it was at a time he was enjoying his life, working as a professional sailor, enjoying his life in Florida–I said, "Come on, Andy, what are you doing? You're wasting your time." I admit I've always regretted that. For me, it was always natural to carry on my father's real estate business.

(He drinks from his glass of water.)

But maybe it's not so easy for the eldest to, right? (aside) I always felt he was defending my mother from something. (Then to the protestor) But you, speaking about my brother, my wife? To trespass here, with your insults. I should have them charge you with trespassing. Little you know you've provided us here with just one more example of what we, what our country, is up against. That there is nothing the rabble media won't stoop to. Nor stories they are willing to plant. It's character assassination. Presidential harassment. ...Escort him out. See that Intelligence runs his record. And next time, son, believe me, should you ever again disrupt such a beautiful event as this one, here or elsewhere, we will be having a very, very different conversation.

(The Protestor is spirited away. Cadmus sits again and returns to eating, smiling, acting unfazed. But the atmosphere is unsettled.)

Scene Two

Speaker Meadows is in his hotel room, still in formal clothes, but tie loosened. The room features two plush purple chairs. A small round walnut table is between the two chairs. A well stocked bar is house left. The TV is running in the background with clips from that evening's dinner/rally on the screen. Rain and thunder is heard. Standing (facing us), he appears to be staring out the window. Sips a glass of scotch on the rocks.

MEADOWS (aloud to himself)

While it is true there are barbarians at the gate who are not us, there are also barbarians at the gate who are us. America coming apart. Or is it that I'm looking back, the seam seeming to spread wider the longer I live? I appear to stand on a mountain I climbed with my tribe, way before this President took office. Cadmus our savior? At last someone whose anti-immigration, anti- affirmative action, anti-abortion, will fight for lower taxes. But must one admit he is "unfit"? His attempts to redefine or expand the Presidency– through confession, tweets, rhetoric–crippled by the sick obsession with repealing his predecessor's legacy. Which only undermines his own. And this obsession with measuring his accomplishments, as if measuring his own body, his own equipment! Even his own good health he makes a big deal of–health is something shared by many and yet he makes it an issue of pride, displays his vanity. He claims to be more healthy, healthier than normal health itself, a kind of trans-health, if you will, as if half way to what Stuart called the Ubermensch. Not to mention plastering his name on towers, like this one.

(Sips his drink, ponders)

But perhaps it is all for the nation. He wants Americans to look not to other strong leaders or to history, neither over there or back, rather to take pride in our own health, our national strengths, putting our best foot forward. "America First." He wants to represent the health of the nation, our exceptionalism. I'm with him with Israel and against picture-hating Islam...this storm turns the news feed in something that looks like Arabic! With him when he speaks in favor of coal miners and construction workers–the pain of factory closings spreads across the rust belt, and grain belt, that country of my heart. Yet in the end he is not my populist, if a populist is what is called for at this juncture. (Staring more intently out the window) My, quite a storm. Like a preview to July 4th celebrations.

(There is a thunderous knock on the door. Meadows clicks off the TV. He opens the door to find Cadmus standing there with the two Secret Service agents. The President is dressed just as before, his tie still straight.)

CADMUS

Jim.

MEADOWS

Mr. President?

CADMUS (walking in)

May I come in?

MEADOWS

Of course, sir.

> (Cadmus closes the door behind him, leaving the agents in the hall.)

CADMUS

Thank you. I'm Richard right now, Jim, no "Mr. President." And I'm riled up.

MEADOWS (remaining cool)

I'd offer you a drink, Richard, but I know you don't imbibe. Too bad, the bar is surely free for you.

CADMUS

Freshen yours. ...We have something to iron out and it might take a while.

MEADOWS

I'm good. (Then) Please sit here, near the window.

> (The men are still standing and peer out the window, Cadmus momentarily distracted from his mission.)

CADMUS

Quite a view, isn't it? Especially after a rain. I put all of myself into this hotel. It required a tremendous amount of work, of deal making. I insisted on everything being done right, at the highest level. I wanted something unique and monumental. The location was the starting point. And then I knew we needed a really big building, a really tall one. From the start, size was a top priority. We wanted a building that stood out and one that allowed for these views, the New York Harbor—the lights ticking there like stars on the water, see that?—the really unparalleled view of Central Park....

> (Cadmus suddenly sits. He sits forward on the chair, and when Meadows sits, Cadmus leans toward him.)

Jim, these leaks are killing us. Something has got to be done. I can't have it, anymore than I'd stand for a leaky building. I won't have it. I'm not saying you or anyone of your aides is responsible—but I'm telling you other people are saying it. I don't know for sure where the leaks are coming from, whether it's Congress or some agency—of course the media is on it—but I'm going to put an end to it, believe me, that boy today knew our policy before it had even been announced. We can't have that. His other claims were too damnedly outrageous to be taken seriously—Basia, my sister, can you believe that! But since he knew one thing you have to wonder what else he knows.

MEADOWS

I assure you, Mr. President...

CADMUS

Richard.

MEADOWS

Richard, I'm not the source of the leaks. And I feel confident in saying no one on my staff is responsible.

CADMUS

I'm not saying you are, Jim. But other people are saying it.

MEADOWS

It could be someone close to you. Someone in the Cabinet.

CADMUS

In the White House? Impossible. Unthinkable. You know I expect loyalty, demand it. We must stick together. Trust each other. The opposition will use every little split in our party to their advantage, you know that.

MEADOWS

You are planning on splitting up families who arrive at the border?

CADMUS

I don't want to do it, I love children, you know that—there's nothing more important than family—but stopping border crossings has to happen. It just has to. We've got to find a way of discouraging people from making the trek to America, Jim, from thinking once they get here everything will be fine. We've just got to. I know conditions in some of those shit-hole places are rough, very tough, but we can't take all of these people in. We've run out of room. We can't have people dragging behind them the whole damn extended family. We need great people coming into our country.

MEADOWS

But, sir, families? There is nothing more American.

CADMUS

But it's got to be legal. Orderly. Done beautifully. Thousands have waited in line legally, for years in some cases—is anyone concerned for them? Do you hear news reports on them, thousands that have waited for years for reunion with their loved ones? And someone else just cuts in line. People wait in line at a sporting event, maybe an hour, and someone else just tries to cut in line. Or in traffic. What about Americans killed by aliens? It happens everyday, one of our own cut down by an illegal. They say illegals commit fewer crimes than normal immigrants. That's the logic of the Left. But what if it were your own daughter? Or son? Killed by someone who wasn't even supposed to be in the country. No, the media is very unfair, very, very unfair. I doubt any entering President has been treated so unfairly by the press as have I. I'm sure no one has.

MEADOWS

I do agree with you there, it's really unprecedented.

(Meadows shakes his empty glass.)

May I?

(Suddenly there is a crack of thunder.)

CADMUS

Who am I to argue with the gods!

(The two men enjoy a laugh.)

(Back to familiar things) But that stuffs not good for you, you know. Oh, it's okay in moderation. But you heard me speak about my brother today.

MEADOWS

I did.

(Having freshened his drink, Meadows sits again.)

CADMUS

That really caught me off guard. Not a day goes by that I don't think of Andy. The other stuff...amazing the stuff people make up just for a little publicity.

(Cadmus sees Meadow's raised eyebrow.)

Don't look at me like that, Jim, I'm not like that. I'm all for publicity, good or bad, but good is better–even if sometimes bad is better than none. Yes, I enhance, dramatize a bit. You're selling people on possibility, a bit of a fantasy, then you try and make it happen. You work very, very hard to make it happen. We're going to make America beautiful again, believe me.

MEADOWS

I'm with you there, too, Mr. President.

CADMUS

But the leaks, the leaking has got to stop.

MEADOWS

I do advise against separating families.

CADMUS (nonresponsive)

I put great faith in personal relationships, you know. We Greeks place a high value on friendship. I need you to put together a committee to investigate leaking in Congress, many times, as you know, it's classified material. Right to the media. Right to the damned, failing Times. You know the architectural critic at The Times wrote a positive review of this building–and why not?–and it made all the difference in getting city approval, both from the zoning commission and the public. What power they have, The Times. Now they're a thorn in my side. The Post no better.

MEADOWS

I can't entirely agree with you about The Times and The Post. Though you have to wonder what they choose to cover and what they don't. What they don't is just as important.

CADMUS (rising, pacing, looking out the window)

That's what I'm saying. We won the election that's the important thing. No one thought the country would elect a Greek–but of course I emphasized my mother's Scottish side and my Presbyterian background! No one thought we'd win, no one did. I'm saying, Jim, it's unfair to our own citizens, these porous borders. My aide, Stuart–I saw you chatting with him–a fine young man, scratch golfer–said everybody thinks of Rousseau, the philosopher–was he French?–as a Romantic, but that he was very patriotic, admired Sparta as a warrior-state, suspicious of its neighbors, that foreigners are merely men, not citizens, nothing in the eyes of a patriot–something to that effect. I'm a Romantic. Romantics are actually the true patriots. The true nationalists.

                    MEADOWS (standing his ground)
But I don't recommend separating families. The public won't stand for it. Think of the optics–sounds–of children ripped away from their mother's arms. You'd be shooting yourself in the foot. And it's the wrong thing to do, too.

                              (Cadmus is about the respond when there is
                              a knock–a softer one–on the door.)

                    MEADOWS
Shall I get it, sir?

                              (Cadmus goes toward the door.)

                    CADMUS (letting down his guard)
I suppose it's for me. Not a minute's peace when you are President.

                              (He opens the door to his wife, Basia, the
                              Secret Service on each side of her like sentries.
                              She is blond, beautiful. Other than being fe-
                              male, and much younger, she looks a lot like
                              him. However, she has an Eastern-European
                              accent.)

Basia?

BASIA

Please forgive me. I don't mean to interrupt.

(Meadows sets down his drink and rises.)

CADMUS (to Basia)

You know Speaker Meadows.

(Meadows holds out his hand and he and Basia shake.)

MEADOWS

Nice to see you again.

BASIA

I'm sorry to interrupt.

MEADOWS (genially)

Just in time. Your husband was giving me a grilling.

BASIA

Oh, he is like tyrant.

CADMUS

See. Even bad press from my wife.

BASIA

It's Richie. Nothing serious...but, but, do you think you can come, Richard? It's important, darling.

CADMUS

Of course. (To Meadows) I'm at her beck and call. (winks) Please excuse us, Jim. Think about what I've said, will you? Can't have a leaking ship of state either.

(The men share a laugh.)

CADMUS

Goodnight then. We're flying back to the White House later tonight. We'll see you back on the Hill after the 4th. Hope you've enjoyed your stay here.

MEADOWS

Very much so, Mr. President. Good evening, First Lady. Basia.

>(Cadmus and Basia exit. Meadows pours another drink from the bar, then sits in the chair that Cadmus was previously sitting in.)

How much longer can I hold my tongue?

>(He drinks. Takes his cell phone from his pocket.)

I hope the President has enough sense to use a secure line.

>(Dials a number. Then...)

Oh, sorry, I meant to ring Langford. (A pause) Oh, his aide, Olivia. Nice to speak with you Miss Wright. Please tell Joe to call me when he's free. (A pause). Thank you, Miss Wright. (Pause) Olivia. (Pause) Yes, I was just speaking to the President about just that, how beautiful the skyline is after a good rain. (Pause) Yes, sometime on Capitol Hill I'm sure.(pause) Goodnight.

Scene Three

A similar hotel room. Two plush chairs and a table toward the front of the stage. But in this room we can see the corner of the bed, on which lies an open suitcase. Cadmus sits in one chair and Richie, a spittin' image of his father, in the other.

Basia stands nearby. The TV is running in the background, tuned to the weather. Richie appears shaken, as if he has been crying.

BASIA

Tell your father, Richie. Please.

RICHIE

I don't want to bother Daddy.

CADMUS

My father was a busy man, but he always made time for me when I was a boy. Your grandfather Cadmus was a great man, Richie. A great success. He was the King of Queens, we used to say. A real estate genius. I grew up with all kinds of people in Queens. Greek, Italian, Jewish. And then I took on snobby Manhattan. He was a great father to me.

RICHIE

I know, Daddy. I remember going for a walk with Grandpa on the boardwalk, in Atlantic City, and how I walked off when he'd turned his head for a second–I must have been four or five. On Steel Pier. I remember the sound of the waves crashing beneath the pier, like a crowd roaring. And could also hear his panicked voice as he called out to me, but I kept playing hide and seek. I hid behind a blue horse on the old carousel, which wasn't in operation before you restored it.

CADMUS

Such a beautiful carousel.

RICHIE

A few minutes later I saw the police swarming the boardwalk. I came out and told them they should arrest me. I wanted to be arrested. I felt guilty for fooling Grandpa that way. He hugged me so tight. After that, he was super-conscientious with me, almost strict.

CADMUS

What a vocabulary you have, Richie. I'm so proud. (Reminiscently)Yes, he could be strict. A martinet. But he was a real man, formidable, what Jews call a mensch.

BASIA (as if interrupting)

Richie! It's okay, tell him. (Turns to Cadmus) He was bullied at school today.

CADMUS (continuing as if to himself)

...Not at all an easy legacy to live up to. (Then back to present) You were? Bullied? I'm sorry, Rich. ...Those things happen. What happened? Stand up for yourself. Outsmart them. Out play them. It's time, anyway, you two moved into the White House. People are starting to talk—"Why hasn't she moved to Washington?" I've never thought highly of that school anyway.

BASIA

You know we are coming soon. I just wanted him to finish elementary school year here.

CADMUS

It's finished. I want you two near. I miss you both. Remember how it was—we were a team.

BASIA

We still are.

CADMUS

I scarcely know these Washingtonians. I don't like most either. They're not our kind. It's not like dealing with businessman. American businessman, in any case. The Chinese are all business. They don't come in and say, "How the wife? The kids?" They sit down and say, "Let's deal."

BASIA (interrupting)

They told him...I can hardly say...they said, the kids at school today—right, Richie?

RICHIE

Some did.

BASIA

...that I was...not only your wife.

CADMUS

Not only?

BASIA (pacing, then)

Your sister. That I was your sister, too.

RICHIE

That you and Mama look alike, they said.

CADMUS (dismissive, yet enraged)

Oh, that nonsense. When did this rumor start?

BASIA

You've heard of this?

CADMUS

Just tonight. Some lunatic protesting...success...broke into our get-together, our rally, tonight. Made all kinds of wild accusations.

BASIA

What else did he say?

CADMUS

He claimed we are separating families at the border.

BASIA

Separating mothers and children? Are you? Are we doing this?

          CADMUS (dissembling)

We would have the right to if we decided to. (Then) Let's get packed. I'm sorry to hear about what happened, Richie. I know you're man enough to take it. There are always some who can't stand to see anyone...succeed. And you, top of your class, a brilliant student like your Uncle Steve, and with your father president, you're bound to get more than your share of jealousy, envy. (With one more glance out the window) At least the skies have cleared for our flight back.

          (There are three knocks on the door.)

What now?

          (Cadmus rises, opens the door. Jack, one of
          the Secret Service agents, enters.)

          JACK

Mr. President, an aide is here to speak to you. From Homeland Security.

          CADMUS

At this hour?

          JACK

Yes, sir.

          CADMUS

Send him in, Jack.

          JACK

Her, sir.

          CADMUS (slightly annoyed)

Yes, yes, her.

JACK

A Miss Wright.

CADMUS

Of course. She works for Langford in DHS. I recommended her.

> (A young attractive blond enters. She looks
> like Basia. Jack exits.)

OLIVIA

Mr. President. First Lady.

CADMUS

Hello, Miss Wright. This is Richie. Richie, Miss Wright.

OLIVIA

Nice to meet you in person, Richie.

RICHIE (rising, excited)

Thank you, mam. Nice to make your acquaintance.

> (They shake hands. The four remain stand-
> ing, Basia and Olivia close to each other, ap-
> pearing almost like sisters.)

CADMUS

What brings you all the way from Washington on such a stormy night, Miss Wright? Your hair is still wet.

OLIVIA

Is it okay to speak here openly, sir? Is this location secure?

CADMUS

This penthouse, yes. I made sure of that even before I became President. It's soundproof.

OLIVIA (looking at Basia and Richie)

It's something that can't get out. Well, one thing is, the other is good news.

CADMUS

They are family. It's safe. (To Richie) But son, it would be best if you leave. Jack will go with you.

BASIA

It will be just a moment, Richie.

RICHIE

Must I? I've only just met Miss Wright.

CADMUS (a short laugh)

You'll see her again.

(Richie exits.)

CADMUS

So what is it, please, Miss Wright?

OLIVIA

Would you prefer the bad news or the good news first, sir?

CADMUS

The bad. One always has to be strong enough to face bad news. Not to mention fake.

OLIVIA

I was sent on this mission by Secretary Langford.

CADMUS

Langford, he's doing a fine job over there at Homeland. (A bit flirtatious, Basia watching him) You, too, I'm sure.

(Olivia fidgets.)

OLIVIA

A child has been found, sir. An immigrant child. One separated from his mother. We think the boy is Guatemalan.

CADMUS

He's alive then. Found where?

OLIVIA

On the doorstep of the White House.

CADMUS

The White House? What? How is that possible? That's impossible. Unthinkable. No person, especially an illegal could wind up on the doorstep of the White House—except maybe my predecessor. Where was the Secret Service?

OLIVIA

Many are here at the hotel, sir. But I don't know how this could have happened.

CADMUS

A detail was left behind?

OLIVIA

Of course, sir. A Secret Service agent found the child.

CADMUS

But what about the security cameras?

OLIVIA

The man was camouflaged. We can tell it was a he. Homeland is working on it.

CADMUS

Working on it? I want answers.

OLIVIA

Yes, sir.

BASIA (in action mode)

How old is the boy?

OLIVIA

Not yet two, we think.

CADMUS (curious, even tender)

My god, a small child. He can walk? Talk?

OLIVIA

Both. But only speaks a few words. In Spanish, sir.

CADMUS

What's the Spanish word for "invasion."

OLIVIA

Sir?

CADMUS

Never mind. ...Is he well taken care of?

OLIVIA

Yes, sir. He's in the White House. But no one except that one agent and one nurse—and Secretary Langford, and myself of course—knows of him. Not yet.

CADMUS

Keep him hid. (aside) Only one person is necessary to blow the whole cover. (Then) No one else must know. That agent will be handsomely compensated.

OLIVIA

It is sure to leak out, Mr. President. And soon I expect.

CADMUS (sheepishly looking at Basia and Richie)

He must be kept hid until after the celebrations of the 4th tomorrow. The optics would be a disaster. There's the midterm elections to think of. We might lose the House and just might lose our wall. (To Olivia) There's a crisis at the border! The opposition turns a blind eye! How on God's earth did this boy get here? If we had a wall...(half to himself) would that be enough? (Then forcefully) Find out the boy's identity–do we know the mother? The father?

OLIVIA

We don't. The boy can't tell us anything. I know Spanish and I can't get anything useful out of him. He seems, I'm afraid to say, traumatized. Bewildered.

CADMUS

That at least is understandable. Children are vulnerable. ..And yet like buoys bob up again.

OLIVIA

Yes, sir, normally.

BASIA (taking charge, stepping between them)

We must hurry. I will take care of him.

CADMUS

You? You're the First Lady. And you have Richie to look after.

BASIA

Richie can help me. But no one must know until his parents are found. Until he is reunited with parents or parent. The President is right.

OLIVIA

They may already be deported, mam. It's a possibility.

BASIA

Find them. Run a DNA test on the boy. Spare nothing. The boy must be reunited with his parents as soon as possible. A child needs his parents. He must be protected from the press, too. From wild suppositions. Some might even insinuate that he's a "love child."

CADMUS

Yes, she's right—the media would run wild with this, as no doubt are already doing after tonight's...debacle.

OLIVIA

Tonight's debacle, sir?

CADMUS

A protestor interrupted our dinner. You'll hear about it soon enough. As for this—isn't it so, as Shakespeare said, "Troubles come not as single spies but in battalions"? I took a Shakespeare class at MIT, got an "A. I have a very big...you know what. The opposition, they sadly would consider this unfortunate boy's story manna from heaven. A gift.

OLIVIA

No doubt.

CADMUS

They care for nothing but power. (sighing) But what was the good news, Miss Wright? We could use some about now, believe me.

OLIVIA

It's shocking news but wonderful, I think. Secretary Langford reports–he learned this as a result of the investigation into your...wealth.

CADMUS

There was no collusion with foreign banks. None!

OLIVIA

Yes, sir. Of course, sir. But at least the investigation has turned up one piece of good news. Our First Lady was actually born here in the U.S.A.

CADMUS (incredulous)

What did you say?

(Cadmus and Basia exchange fearful looks. Then they both look at Richie. Richie is confused by it.)

OLIVIA (cheerfully)

A birth certificate has been found!

CADMUS

Found? I saw her birth certificate when we married. (Addressing Basia as if betrayed) Do you know anything of this?

BASIA (defensive)

Not really. But I don't want to discuss this right now, Richard. In private. I can explain.

OLIVIA

I'm sorry. I thought it would be good news.

CADMUS (covering)

Of course, Miss Wright, it is. Just surprising. Shocking, I'm sure you can imagine. Basia a native- born American. Let's just keep it, also, between us right now. Only Langford knows, right?

OLIVIA

I believe so.

CADMUS

Good.

BASIA (to Miss Wright)

We must pack quickly.

OLIVIA

Of course. I will go now. I will see you soon, at the White House. I'm taking a red-eye.

CADMUS (calculating)

You can—should—fly with us, Olivia. I've completely remodeled Air Force One. You'll love it.

BLACKOUT

END OF ACT ONE

Act Two

July 4. The Oval Office in the White House. In the middle is a massive square desk and a leather desk chair. A window is directly behind the desk. A July 4th banner is draped from the window.

On either sides of the window stand two American flags. Two chairs are situated on either side of the desk facing the window. There are also two couches facing each other. Meadows paces, occasionally looking out the window.

MEADOWS (aloud to himself)
I imagine this White House is something of a disappointment to him, a man who loves not so much houses as resorts. Country clubs. Castles. Not even the bourgeois domicile dream of a lot next to a golf course would be enough. He builds his own course–I fear he desires to build his own country. Like the one he grew up in. In late life, people recreate their childhoods no matter what that childhood was like, it seems–for him it must be memories of his daddy's country club in Queens, or of Central Park, or maybe the fields of Culver Military Academy, where I know he thrived–among loyal friends. I suspect he's seeking that frontier again. Combat for him is that, the early past, back when things were competitive, fun, as Stuart says. (Peering out the window) But for me, a cornfield is more beautiful than Central Park, a river more beautiful than an ocean. Our minds are shaped by the geography of our childhood. By instinct, I'm Jeffersonian–I'll meet the Federalist in the street. But who I am to say, of him, he is unfit when he is fitting himself into a different past? Childhood is so vivid, it is hard to imagine any other than our own. Whose to say the agrarian past is not passe? And aren't we all, on this side of the aisle particularly, desiring, like Oedipus, to go home, home to an earlier version of America. Shouldn't I, like my comrades, let the lion-headed man then speak for me? Surely I can

work with him—and object when there's an overreach. He's never seen a horizon—bottled in, he just builds higher. No doubt he misses his New York connections—funny that he seems to have latched on to me as a confidant. I suppose he doesn't feel he can trust Langford. That son-of-a-bitch never returned my call! (Looks at the desk) I wonder if he left me here alone in Oval Office on purpose? It certainly breaks protocol.

(Cadmus enters, shakes Meadows' hand)

CADMUS

Didn't think I'd see you so soon again, Jim. Sorry to ruin your Iowa weekend. Love the state. Your people were very, very good to me in the primary and during the election, weren't they? (Ribbingly) My coattails served you well, didn't they?

MEADOWS

They did, Mr. President.

(Cadmus sits in his seat behind the presidential desk. Before Meadows can sit, Cadmus stands.)

CADMUS

On the other hand, let's drag these chairs over here.

(They take the chairs on either side of the desk, sit down close to each other in the middle of the stage, facing us.)

I've got something important to discuss with you. Even more important than the leaking, but it's something, again, that can't be leaked. An inexplicable thing has happened and I need your counsel, your help. And loyalty. I think someone is out to—I'll be honest, I don't know whom.... Fact is, a child was left on the doorstep of this house late last night.

MEADOWS

My god, the White House?

CADMUS

I know, impossible, isn't it? When they tell you something was left on your door-step, you think they mean metaphorically. It's crazy. It has to be some sort of inside job. A set-up. There are people here in the Deep State who don't want me to succeed, don't like change. And not just the career politicians like yourself... sorry, I have to tell the truth as I see it...but deep state actors, that's what we have to fear.

MEADOWS

Anything's possible, sir. ...

CADMUS

Richard.

MEADOWS

Richard. ...But how could a child wind up here?

CADMUS

He's an illegal, we assume. Guatemalan, we think. Two years old. He cries for his mom most of the time. I don't blame him for that. I'm pro-child, Jim, you know that. Anti-abortion, like you. We are on the same side.

MEADOWS

No one knows he's here?

CADMUS

Only a very few people. Basia is personally taking care of him. I've got Homeland working on the case. Priority. But they don't know the boy is here, in the White House. Except Langford, he knows. And his aide, Miss Wright. I still can't be-lieve this is happening. I think I'm half in denial, to tell you the truth. Though as for that, I sometimes can't, to begin with, believe that I live in the White House. (More rhetorical) At the same time I see it all as my destiny. To do something great for the country. I've been preparing all my life for this without knowing it. A President is a dealmaker. But he's got to think big. Churchill said: "Foolish perhaps. But I play for high stakes." Think long-term. Plan. Then take risks. Everyone thinks I'm impulsive. But I'm as stable as they come. That's always been one of my strengths. That, and my instincts.

MEADOWS

My god, a boy left like that. How terrible. Let me be frank, Richard, this separating children could bring down your presidency. Not to mention echo down through history—just as a child's history, the ghosts of his past, inescapably alters the lives of his progeny. That's another reason for not separating children from their parents. Think of the fathers who are torn from their children during divorce. That trauma never leaves father or child. I scarcely ever saw my father after my parents divorced. I especially wanted him there at my baseball games. I was good athlete back then. A lefty.

CADMUS

Not too left, I hope. I was a heck of an athlete, too.

MEADOWS

You were lucky to have your father.

CADMUS (reminiscent)

Yes, he was a great man. A rock. My mother, too, both steady as a rock. (Then) I'm sorry to hear it wasn't the same for you.

MEADOWS

My mother was great. But I'll admit I always resented her for keeping my father from me. (He turns away, looks out the window. Then back at Cadmus.) This child, having him here, it's potentially more explosive than even the investigation into foreign ties.

CADMUS

There's no bank fraud. Nothing. None.

MEADOWS

I believe that...Richard. But you see, right, that this separating children plays into those suspicions and to you having married a foreigner?

CADMUS

She was a citizen by then.

MEADOWS

But she came here, some say—I'm not saying it, but some have—under mysterious circumstances.

CADMUS

It's no mystery. She first came here as a model. On a special visa.

MEADOWS

The "Einstein" visa?

CADMUS (quickly)

Anyway, I'm not worried about that part anymore. The visa. Her origins. It's been cleared up. She...

(He stops himself from saying more. Stands. Looks out the window. Meadows waits. Cadmus sits back down. Leans in.)

Jim, about the child.

MEADOWS

Sir?

CADMUS

There are some two thousand children in similar circumstances.

MEADOWS (shocked, but holding it in check)

Two thousand? My god. How could this happen?

CADMUS

I'd planned to formally announce our "Zero Tolerance" policy right after the 4th–I ordered the Attorney General to begin its implementation three months ago. We had to be tough, very tough. As you know, a caravan of illegals was headed our way. Guatemalans, El Salvadorians, Mexicans, you name it. And you know what they bring with them–drugs, crime, a lot of mouths to feed. But now that the word has leaked out about the policy–and as you certainly know, there's already been a hew and cry in the media this morning–and with the boy here– I've decided I have no choice, no choice, but to end the policy. And to not to say anything about it, like it never officially existed–though to tell you the truth, I'm not sure I'll be able to shake this boy's trauma from my dreams. (Back to business) But I think I can claim it was already the policy of my predecessor in any case. It was, even if they never acted on it.

MEADOWS

Where do I fit in?

CADMUS

Immediately bring to the floor immigration legislation? Try to make a deal. That's what's needed at this moment. That's what I need from you.

MEADOWS

We don't have the votes for any proposal right now, as you know. There's no way to thread that needle. The Far Right and Far Left each have the power to hold us hostage. The Left won't accept your border wall, the Right a path to citizenship for the undocumented.

CADMUS

Illegals, not "undocumented," Jim. They're in the country illegally. But I'll tell you, when people say things can't be done, I don't accept it. The important thing right now, in any case, is that we give the impression that we are working on immigration, are close to a deal. I'll include something about it, obliquely, in my speech today, at the festivities. It will buy us some time.

MEADOWS

Not much, I'm afraid.

CADMUS

Time to think of what to do next.

MEADOWS

What do you plan to do with the boy?

CADMUS

Keep him hid, in the White House, for today. Then spirit him away somewhere tomorrow.

MEADOWS

If it were to ever get out, leak, be disclosed, that you hid him, I fear the worst. Don't underestimate the opposition.

CADMUS

It won't get out. I'm expecting a report on his DNA and his relatives later today. Basia is taking care of that.

MEADOWS

The First Lady?

CADMUS

Yes, with Langford, Olivia. If we can find the parents, we will fly them here immediately. Turn it all around. Show that we've been taking care of a boy that someone callously left on the White House doorstep. Leave it to me. I know how to change the perspective, the subject. It's called a Red Herring. Do you fish, Jim?

MEADOWS

Did you know that comes from using a fish to train dogs, so they wouldn't be thrown off the scent?

CADMUS (nonresponsive)

One thing my father didn't do was take me fishing. It wasn't until I got to Culver that I got to really enjoy the outdoors. Except for golf, there was always golf. I grew up playing on the stairs, not in a yard. (Abruptly) I know I can trust you, Jim, at Culver I saw the Midwest first hand. Honest people. I know you're loyal...I've made it worthwhile for the others who know about the boy. Jack, my Secret Service, for instance.It's good to be filthy rich in circumstances like this. You know how they'll talk about a pitcher with filthy stuff? Unhittable?

MEADOWS (anxious to leave)

I'll see what I can do, Mr. President. I have a meeting with the Freedom Caucus tomorrow, see if I can bring them round to at least say they will discuss a path to citizenship. I'll be back in touch. I'm not sure I'd bring up immigration today when you speak, except very obliquely.

CADMUS

I won your state by double-digits, right?

MEADOWS (a bit resentfully)

Right.

CADMUS

Great people, Iowans.

(Cadmus rises. Meadows follows suit. The two men shake hands. Meadows exits.

Cadmus sits back down at his desk. He picks
up the phone.)

Get me, Langford. ...No, check that.

(He ponders. Sets the phone down.)

Could it be Langford? Could be anyone. Even Meadows.

(He picks up the phone again.)

Adams. Get me Stuart Adams. (Aside) I need something on Meadows. His
drinking maybe. And something on Langford. There's got to be something. His
predecessor was a cross-dresser for God's sake.

Scene Five

The Presidential bedroom in the White House. Cadmus sits at the vanity, comb-
ing his hair. He has on a white shirt, white boxers shorts, and high socks. Basia
moves around the room getting dressed. She is in underwear. They can scarcely
bear to look at each other.

CADMUS (looking at her through the
mirror)

How is the boy doing?

BASIA

He is okay. He won't say much. Seems very confused. He reminds me so much
of Richie when he was young...I suppose any young boy would. But we can't risk
any knowledge getting out. You must be careful what you say publicly, darling.
We don't yet know our way around here. The real rules of the game. You have to
be from somewhere else to know what you don't know sometimes, darling. You
can't just shoot your mouth off.

CADMUS (offended, swiveling around to look at her)

I don't just shoot off my mouth, Basia. There's a method to it. Anyway, I believe in being myself no matter where I am. (Then into the mirror) Richie is okay? Has he said anything?

BASIA

He's very upset, I think. There's so much pressure on him. And now this...this wild speculation. All the wolves coming down from the mountains into the village.

CADMUS (swiveling around again)

So are you going to tell me about your childhood? Have you seen your birth certificate, the real one?

BASIA

I have not seen it.

CADMUS

I want to see it! I'm going to call Langford.

BASIA

I beg you not to pursue that further, Richard. It can't do good. Certainly not for Richie. Nothing can be changed.

CADMUS (bewildered)

What was the birth certificate I saw?

BASIA

I have no idea. I'm in shock really—that my father, whom I loved, might not be my father after all. This is not political to me.

CADMUS (as if to the fates)

Neither him nor your mother alive to clear things up!

BASIA

Don't speak ill of the dead, Richard. Have I ever said a bad word about your brother?

CADMUS

My brother again. I wonder what he knew! (Accusatory, stands up, looking at her directly) ...Didn't you hear anything about your father not being your birth father? *Before* we married.

BASIA (half to herself)

Not that I paid attention to. My grandmother used to joke–in Czech–about me being an American girl. But I thought she was teasing me about being a fashionista. Anyway, she was half-senile. My mother said don't pay attention to what she says. When we married, my stepfather was dead, as you know. Nor did I feel free to ask my mother. You understand what that would mean–in my culture. Suggesting she had an affair. For women, Russian Orthodox women, it simply wasn't done. Wasn't tolerated. Your father was Greek Orthodox...oh god, do you think they met through...no, impossible (Now more direct) It couldn't be...your father. Richard. It couldn't. My mother was at our wedding...my beautiful white dress–remember, it cost a fortune–still hangs in our closet.

CADMUS

But don't forget my father wasn't at the wedding. He was at my first two but not ours. Nor was my mother. I regret that both died too early to see me, at last, form a happy marriage. The necessary conjunction of sky and earth that all need. But now? Where is that happiness? I put all my trust in you.

BASIA

My mother would have said something. Not all the money and power in marrying you offered to us would have kept my mother from saying something. She was religious...as they come, as Americans say. She would have feared...she would have never done such a thing to me. Betrayed me. Would have feared burning in...unless?

CADMUS

Unless what?

BASIA (half to herself)

Unless she thought it was the best way of covering it up? The transgression. (Almost in admiration) How clever Mother was. No one would suspect...

CADMUS

My father could never have cheated on my mother. Besides, there are millions of Americans that could be your father. It's a big country. It's impossible, unthinkable, that we could be...

BASIA

Don't say it, please. No longer think about it. It's not possible, Richard.

CADMUS

Siblings. You see I must know for sure. I must. Funny, in Ancient Greece and Rome it was not unusual among the powerful for brother and sister to bed. When you said my name just now, it sounded different, like a voice from another time. If it turns out to be true, we will keep it secret. We can, we will continue!

> (He rises from his chair and goes toward her. He holds her. Goes to kiss her.)

BASIA (softly, half-resisting)

No! ...No, Cadmus.

> (He kisses her cheek. Her breasts. Then goes for her lips. Then she more forcefully.)

No!

> (She tears herself away from him.)

BASIA

I'd rather I were dead!

(She runs from the room, half-dressed. He starts after her, but then stops.)

CADMUS

Come back, Basia!

(Cadmus appears disoriented. He staggers back to the vanity, sits, and stares at himself in the mirror.)

Am I a criminal? Was my father a philanderer? (He strokes his hair.) But, if so, does that not makes us even more alike, more father and son than ever? He never missed a single one of my football games.

(After a pause, he takes a blue tie from the rack, looks at it as if he'd never seen a tie before, then drapes it around his neck. Pauses again. Then ties it neatly. Stands. Puts on his tux pants. Regroups. As if out of habit, admires himself in the mirror. An agent knocks three times and enters.)

Come in.

(He finishes dressing while speaking to Jack.)

JACK

Mr. President, Miss Wright is here.

CADMUS

Show her in. (Aside, as Jack goes to the door) Even he could be a whistleblower.

(Olivia enters in red ball dress.)

CADMUS (pushing his concerns aside, almost a shtick)

How stunning you look, O. Do you mind if I call you "O"? I like nicknames, as you know–mostly as insults. I've come up with some good ones lately, don't you think–"Sacajawea" is my favorite, for that phony Sen. Melanie Carson who claimed on her entrance application to Harvard that she was part Indian. She's about as Indian as the Washington Redskins. Your boss, Langford, didn't take too kindly to my calling him "Sangfroid" though, as if I was commenting on his lack of urgency about border security. But I was only remarking on his coolness.

OLIVIA

He's the last holdover, isn't he?

CADMUS

Of the Mohicans? And he might not last long either.

(Olivia, wide-eyed, is surprised by the suggestion that Langford might be fired.)

OLIVIA (covering)

I do get a kick out of Sacajawea, sir.

CADMUS

I suppose you know I used to run the Miss World pageant. There were many, many very beautiful girls. But none more beautiful than you this evening, O.

OLIVIA (enjoying it)

Thank you, Mr. President. …It's Versace.

CADMUS

Spin around.

OLIVIA

Sir?

CADMUS (rambling)

Oh, don't mind me. I just wanted to get the full effect. I love beauty, Olivia. I can't help myself. You know those Hollywood actresses that cheated to get their children into elite colleges? I despise liberals like them, but I understand their need to have the best. I remember my uncle saying, "If you can't go first class, don't go at all." We all want beauty, don't we? A beautiful building, a beautiful car, a beautiful...wife. Children.

OLIVIA

Is there something wrong, sir?

CADMUS (his best smile)

No.

(She suddenly spins, showing off the dress.)

OLIVIA

How's that?

CADMUS

Wonderful. It's like a Chinese fan. I don't trust the Chinese, but I appreciate their arts.

OLIVIA (professional again)

I have some good news, Mr. President. And also what may be good news.

CADMUS

Again? Well, you choose which first. Everything will come out in the end.

OLIVIA

We think we've matched the boy's DNA to the mother–although not yet reunited them. We think the mother is in a holding center in Los Angeles. Apparently the father is in jail. In the U.S.

CADMUS

See, so many of them are...break the law, believe me. Just coming into our country uninvited is breaking the law. How could we not know for sure the mother?

OLIVIA

I'm embarrassed to say DHS didn't do a good job of documenting the families when they were separated. There's some discrepancies. But you can't argue with DNA.

CADMUS

Yes, it's a game changer. We always held women to a higher standard because a man's got to know if it's his own child. You can't have women running around having someone else's baby. (Stops, realizing what he just said. Regroups) But now, with DNA, we can nail these things down ...do you think it was intentional?

OLIVIA

Intentional, sir?

CADMUS

Those errors. ...But never mind. What's done is done. Maybe they were honest mistakes. Or incompetency.

OLIVIA

The scenes were very difficult, chaotic. Children crying incessantly. There was such confusion, chaos. There were holding pens. What the media calls "cages," as you know. Some kids were crying, others looked simply traumatized, their young faces like smooth pavement. I...oh, I'm sorry, Mr. President, I know it's not what you want to hear. I know your intentions are noble. And it's no excuse, those scenes weren't, for not properly documenting the families.

CADMUS (a bit shaken)

I'm sure it wasn't pleasant. Believe me, my aim is to protect children from parents who bring them unwanted to this country. Sometimes it's not even their own...children. (Back to business) I want to stop parents from even considering such a dangerous, reckless trek to our border. Of course Mexico doesn't want those from Latin America, so they facilitate passage to our country! Some die of hypothermia in route. Some are robbed by the Mexicans. Or raped—even by others in the caravan. And the Mexicans themselves, they are not sending their best across our border, why would they. Most of those entering are criminals. They're dumping criminals, gang members. Some of them are entering from Canada. Or what about those Chinese who overstay their visas?

OLIVIA

Many small colleges depend on the tuition of foreign students.

CADMUS

Still, many Chinese students studying in our country are spies for China—I saw that on TV. The opposition is so naive—they think everyone has the same motives as we do, O. Nothing could be further from the truth...(as if she is not there) thousands of visa cancellations are coming, believe me! ...(then returning to familiar things) You mentioned other news?

OLIVIA

Yes, Mr. President. I suppose you are already aware that at the time we did a DNA test on the boy the First Lady insisted on a DNA test for her. I'm sure she mentioned it.

CADMUS (unconvincingly)

Yes, of course.

OLIVIA

I've brought her results with me.

CADMUS (surprised, fearful)

You have?

OLIVIA

Yes, sir. No one knows the results. It's a sealed envelope. No one except one technician knows, and then of course the results do not have much meaning until they are matched with others.

CADMUS

You can leave the letter with me, O. I'll see that she gets it. I had my own DNA test when I took office. Protocol. Everything around here is protocol. Custom. No one seems to understand the limits of protocol. The limits of being what they call "presidential." It's easy to act presidential, but hard to actually get things done!

OLIVIA

That's certainly true, Mr. President.

(Cadmus looks at her a bit skeptically, won-dering if her deference is calculated.)

CADMUS

If people treat me well, I treat them well, Olivia. But if they try to fool me or are disloy-al, they wind up with the worst enemy they've ever known. I'm sure Langford under-stands that, right? "Presidential" is equivalent to letting people take advantage of you.

OLIVIA (appealing to him)

I like how you redefine things, sir. Rename things.

(He smiles, unable to not respond to praise.)

CADMUS

I'll see you soon at the ball, O. I look forward to it. Enjoy yourself. Our freedom is a great thing—and things could get tough, very very tough very soon. You never know. Its serves no purpose to pretend to know the future.

(Olivia removes the envelope from her purse and places it on the bed as Cadmus watches. She appears to give him a significant look.

Then exits. Cadmus stares at the envelope, picks it up, holding it gently.)

"Confidential." Nothing is confidential to the President.

(Holding the envelope, he sits back down at the vanity table, again looking at himself in the mirror. Stares at the envelope.)

Later. I've got a public to face. A face to meet the faces that you meet, as Dad said.

(He places the unopened envelope in the center vanity drawer.)

(Again, there are three knocks on the door. Jack enters.)

JACK

The limousine is ready, Mr. President.

CADMUS (encouraging himself)

Thank you. It's going to be a beautiful evening, Jack. My favorabilities are through the roof. Please have someone tell the First Lady I've gone ahead.

(He exits with Jack. Moments later Basia enters, surprised to find Cadmus is not there. She is now dressed for the ball, in a stylish black dress. She checks her phone. Reads the message aloud to herself.)

BASIA

"Basia, my love, Olivia arrived with news I was needed at the ballroom for a sound-check. See you there."

> (She sits down at the vanity, and speaks into the mirror.)

I see how he looks at young Olivia. Should I be angry at the natural inclinations of the man—but the disclosure of his affair with that stripper, Melody Stokes, has already caused so much heartache and shame. Caused me such heartache and shame. As it has for our son. And all this, may be but swift omens.

> (She reaches in the drawer and pulls out a hair-brush and begins to brush her hair. She puts on lipstick. Tries out a couple of smiles in the mirror. She goes to replace the brush but notices an envelope. She retrieves it from the drawer.)

"Confidential"? Must be the results.

> (She hesitates, then carefully opens the envelope. She holds up two sheets of paper. She looks at one.)

What, "Richard Cadmus"?

> (She looks at the other sheet.)

Mine?

> (She closely compares the two results. Shaken, she drops the papers to the floor. Rising, walks around distractedly.)

Mother of God! It can't be so. …Is there anyone more hated by God than Basia?

> (But then, she slowly picks up the results from the floor, folds one inside the other, and replaces them inside the envelope. A strange calm having come over her, she sits again, places the envelope back in the drawer, and speaks into the mirror.)

They are one now, like lovers…like family.

> (She takes a long hairpin from the vanity.)

Forgive me, Richie, my beautiful son. But what future is there for you, a freak of nature? Especially when your mother…your aunt…is still alive–a freak, too, for all to see. But perhaps there is always hope for a boy–a girl would be shunned. Forgive me, as well, Richard, dear husband…dear brother. I love you now even more than before. You taught me to always face the truth. The truth is some loves, some shames, are too much to bear. For you, family pride is paramount, I know. Two rushing rivers now meet, the thunderous waters threatening to flood the banks and drown all those in the vicinity. I cannot witness it.

> (She stabs her heart with the hairpin. Blood trickles down the vanity to the floor. Her head falls forward. Her upper body drapes across the vanity.)

Scene Six

A ballroom in the White House. Again government officials and Cadmus' close advisors sit on a dais. However Speaker Meadows is not there. Glasses of red wine, but no food, are set on the dais. At Cadmus's empty spot, in the middle, there is a glass of water and a microphone. There is an additional empty seat to his left. Stuart again sits house left, but this time he is seated next to Olivia. A TV camera is house right. The ballroom resembles the ballroom at the international hotel in New York. A lone Army soldier is standing. He holds a trumpet. As Cadmus enters he plays "Hail to the Chief." All rise. Some applause and pomp.

> (Cadmus stands behind his seat. The music stops.)

CADMUS

Please, at ease. Sit.

> (He sits and the others follow. Seated, Cadmus glances down at Olivia and smiles.)

STUART (toasting to Olivia)

You have the eye of the President, I see.

OLIVIA (spontaneously)

You seem to have his ear, Stuart. That's what I want. There are forces working against our President, it's clear to me now.

STUART

You know something I don't know?

OLIVIA (pulling back, covering)

Oh, I know there is always opposition, especially when someone introduces so much change, and so quickly–I know he rubs many the wrong way–but I *fear* someone or some group is conspiring to bring him down. Even to his knees. I've heard reputable people question his competence. Even his mental competence. That he's schitzo. As I'm sure have you. But they are reading him only in the light of traditional norms–he is really remaking the presidency, from the ground up. He deserves a chance to put his imprint on the job. He is not a government guy.

STUART (toasting)

Cheers to that, O–I heard the President call you that a minute ago–one is indeed glad to at last see a man who despite all those who wish him ill, will not subject himself to censorship, castration, or course correction. He appeared to deconstruct his own application for the position during the campaign. But he knew what he was doing. If consistency is not his forte, so what. (He chuckles, then back in his expository mode.) The muses value performance over verity. Yes, he is not a government guy, rather a civil libertarian, like my dad, who led the fight, in Texas, against the use of red-light cameras. It turned out their lobbyists were hiding the fact that the people behind it all were an off-shore company out to bilk American citizens. It's true, if Cadmus had something on you or the FBI did, he'd use it. You have to protect your own civil liberties, thank god. The nanny state however deep it goes is kaput. Once again you are free to say, do as you like. Personal relations are reestablished as primary.

> (Stuart bats his eyes at her suggestively but also half- mockingly. Drinks. Toasts again.)

To the end of social engineering I say! A remarkable turn of events, isn't it? Aren't we sick of nuance? The President understands that one wins Self-Consciousness in battle. Through action only. But I know you're right, those against him won't stop either, if they have the guts. I tell you this in confidence, O, there's even a resistance afoot right within his, our, own administration. But you already knew that, I expect.

OLIVIA (careful)

I've heard rumors–nothing more.

STUART

The question is should a President be exempt with regard to certain behaviors–financial, sexual, racial–others are held accountable for? A CEO, say, or Hollywood mogul? (Laughingly) Well, the latter, God knows, those snowflakes, should pay the piper for *their* transgressions!

                                  OLIVIA (laughing)

Straight up.

                                STUART (encouraged)

Half their time is spent making mostly lame movies, the other half giving out awards to each other! They just can't deal with Cadmus's much deeper, more profound narcissism, his respect for his own attributes—Emerson said, if I may: "All great men find eternity affirmed in the promise of their faculties"—meantime most in Hollywood would kill to play him. We have in Cadmus a man who won't betray himself, who will accept even destruction to defeat—for the sake of the nation.

                        (Suddenly Cadmus is standing behind them.)

                                CADMUS

Excuse me, Olivia. Stuart.

                        (Both Stuart and Olivia swivel round.)

I need to ask a small favor of Olivia.

                                STUART

Certainly, Mr. President.

                        (Cadmus turns to the soldier.)

                                CADMUS

Do you know "America the Beautiful"? Of course you do. Would you play it, softly?

                                SOLDIER

Yes, sir.

(Cadmus and Olivia move away from
Stuart to speak privately. Stuart eyes them
quizzically.)

OLIVIA

Yes, sir?

CADMUS

I don't want to involve any more Secret Service personnel. Or anyone else. I
wonder would you inquire after my wife...The First Lady. She isn't responding
to texts. She doesn't like leaving...(quietly) the child...in charge of the nurse. Or
Richie either, right now. But I want her to be here when I make my remarks
tonight. It's Independence Day after all. I'll let the Secret Service fellow–Jack–
know that you are on your way.

OLIVIA

Why of course, Mr. President.

CADMUS

Our secret is still secure? The boy.

OLIVIA

No leak that I'm aware of. (She starts to leave) I'll text you in a few minutes.

CADMUS

Use my personal line, O.

OLIVIA

Sir?

CADMUS

The one I gave you. I was in a hurry tonight and grabbed the wrong phone.

OLIVIA (unflinching)

Yes, Mr. President.

> (She departs. Cadmus signals to the trum-
> peter to stop and returns to his seat. Smiles
> broadly—but as always there's a bit of a per-
> formance mixed in—as if overcoming what-
> ever awkwardness a moment may bring.
> Some fireworks are heard.)

CADMUS

Must be the Senate shooting theirs early. Just not that disciplined. Not. Though usually they lag behind.

> (Laughter)

> (He pulls out his phone.)

Forgive me. I keep telling my son Richie to turn off his phone before it takes over his soul and here I am like a banshee.

> (Cadmus puts phone away, looks worried,
> but keeps up a positive front)

CADMUS

Unless the First Lady gets here soon, I'll have to trot out some old material. Speaking of which, how come they got all that marble over there at the Capitol? I guess it's that they want to pretend they're Greek or Roman. We could use a bit of marble here in the White House, I think. I'm the real Greek. You know I like to use crushed marble for the sand traps at my best golf courses. All of my courses are the best though. It's just that some are even more special.

(Moments later he checks a message on his phone. Abruptly rising from his seat, he drops his phone on the floor and knocks over his glass of water. Sets the glass upright again. Looks carefully at the gathered as if for the last time. Then, with tears in his eyes, addresses the assembled.)

Never forget our great country, no matter what. It was never about me, believe me!

(More fireworks are heard. He quickly exits. The assembled stare at each other, speechless. Stuart surreptitiously picks up the phone from the floor.)

Scene Seven

The Oval Office. The July 4th banners have been removed. And now, a vintage liquor cart is in one corner. Meadows stands alone behind the presidential desk, his back to us, staring out the window. He turns and then sits down at the desk. Lifts a phone on his desk.

MEADOWS

Olivia, would you come in, please?

(She enters. She is dressed professionally, but in a sort of schoolgirlish fashion.)

MEADOWS

Adjusting okay to the new role, are you, my dear? Not letting the rumors get to you? How terrible for you to have to see Basia slumped over her vanity...

OLIVIA

We were afraid to move her, touch her. Jack said we shouldn't. It was a sickening sight. A death should be a private affair. But we stood there waiting for Cadmus. And the FBI. Jack took notes.

MEADOWS

So you were there to witness Cadmus's shock and grief.

OLIVIA

He cried out like an animal caught in a trap, Mr. President. I never expected to see him in such a state. Such a proud man he was. Stuart was there too, as you know. I could see he was disbelieving. I tried to keep my cool, even as Cadmus whispered, in his despair: "Chips off the old block."

MEADOWS

What the devil did he mean by that? Though I've always felt he had a chip on his shoulder.

OLIVIA (hesitates, then)

I'm not exactly sure, sir, what he meant.

MEADOWS

Who heard it, besides you and Stuart?

OLIVIA

Just Jack.

MEADOWS

No one else?

OLIVIA

No. The other Secret Service personnel were outside the door.

MEADOWS

For now, certain things must be kept hush-hush, you understand of course. One person is enough for a leak. Did you know Cadmus was using an unsecure phone line? He may have been his own worst enemy as far as leaks go. I have Langford's preliminary report on that and matters more generally, but so far I've only had time to read the executive summary. You trust Langford, do you, Olivia?

OLIVIA (slight hesitation)

I've no real call not to.

MEADOWS (a questioning look, then)

Richie apparently believes the worst about his grandfather, the elder Cadmus, about his philandering. I suppose that's where the absurd rumors came from–Cadmus and Basia siblings! Cadmus thought it was all a plant. Certainly his older brother Andy would have known something–(half to himself) god, maybe he did.

OLIVIA

I try not to think about it. It's gross.

(Meadows suddenly rises and goes to the liquor cart.)

MEADOWS

It's that time of the afternoon. I bought this cart right off a Hollywood lot. It's circa 1940.

(He holds up a whiskey bottle.)

Can I interest you in one?

OLIVIA

I think I could use one, sir. I like Scotch.

MEADOWS

So do I. Straight up?

OLIVIA

Yes, please.

(He pours two drinks.)

MEADOWS

Please sit here to my right, Olivia. My mother was a teetotaler, like many Midwesterners.

(He hands her a drink and sits again. She sips and then sets hers on the edge of the President's desk. He sips his and then sets it on the desk. Then half to himself)

Certainly DNA could provide the answer. But that might require interring Basia's body. How horrible.

OLIVIA (careful)

Secretary Langford sheds no light?

MEADOWS

He's looking into it. The whole thing is kind of amazing to contemplate–a President of the United States married to his half sister–(musingly) though I guess we are all related on some level. ...But it certainly would explain Basia's terrible act. The Secretary and I have agreed to keep everything as I say hush-hush until such time as an investigation can be completed into her death, and other things, so the worst of the rumors can be put to bed....no pun intended. You can add nothing to the report, my dear?

OLIVIA (quickly)

I'm not privy to it. As you know, I resigned immediately.

MEADOWS (sips his drink, then)

How unfortunate for you that the rumor mill–and that damned twenty-four hour news cycle–gives no rest. I would have inquired earlier about you, Olivia, but with all the turmoil these last few days I'm not even unpacked. Not entirely, though part of being President I've quickly learned is that a lot of things are done for you.

OLIVIA

Do not worry, I am adjusting, Mr. President. Of course it's all been a terrible shock. I try not to pay attention to the rumors. I had only a working relationship with former President Cadmus. Whatever they may say.

MEADOWS

Of course. I wouldn't have hired you on if I thought there was anything to all that. To suggestions of...love. Or sex. Unfortunately, there are always stronger forces at work than innocence.

OLIVIA

I appreciate the confidence and will do my best to serve you faithfully, sir. I thought my career in government was over. Your hiring me has put a damper on the rumors, thank heavens.

MEADOWS

That was as I hoped, for your sake, and for mine–and for Cadmus, too. He will need all the help he can get going forward. To lose your wife, and to step down from the Presidency–under pressure–in a short week is really beyond belief. To be hiding an alien boy in the White House and have it be discovered by the public on the very same evening, on July 4th no less–I guess it's what they call a perfect storm. Not to mention the Vice President's terrible faux pas, criticizing Basia's suicide as a threat to the social order, as an attack on the state–and thus his forced resignation. Perhaps it is best the country begins with a clean slate, just as it did nearly 250 years ago. Though we need to find out definitively what precipitated Basia's seemingly blasphemous act. I confess I want to pick your brain on that, at some point later on, O. Do people ever call you that?

OLIVIA

Some have.

MEADOWS

Well, will stick to Olivia. I don't want to be among the "some."

OLIVIA (nervously)

I'm not sure I know much more than do you, sir, about Basia.

MEADOWS (still processing the events)

They seemed a family so blessed with good fortune! Like father, like son, going from success to success—except, I guess we must acknowledge it, not when it came to marriage. And love affairs. An Achilles heal, I guess. Who knows what's yet to come out about Cadmus's many dalliances? Or his father's? (This hangs in the air a moment) And the other, the investigation, the financial probe, may still prove very, very damaging. Ironically, now that he is out of office he's more vulnerable to prosecution. Though I still have, or now have—strange, it's something I have only acquired since Tuesday last—the ability to pardon him, or others. (Half-jokingly) Everyone but myself! (Then musingly) How odd it is to have such power. (Then) But more of that...anon, as they say, Olivia. You can be sure I will protect you. You understand me, right?

OLIVIA

Yes. Thank you, Mr. President.

MEADOWS

At the moment I need your help with my speech. I'm really struggling with it. Embarrassed to be suddenly thrust into the role of President, I guess. Flustered, abashed, chagrined, you name it. Preeminently, I want this speech to sound like me—and certainly not like the former President's speech writers, who are at my disposal for the present. Not that he ever stayed on script.

(They laugh.)

OLIVIA

You can say that again.

(Laugh again.)

MEADOWS (almost conspiratorial)

I'll need to play things close to vest anyway for a while. I am not entirely sure whom I can trust from the current cabinet, so many are still loyal to Cadmus—and others, who knows, may have been, as I suggested, plotting his downfall. But it's good to pass a speech by someone before delivering it, and I feel I can trust you, Olivia. Don't ask me why, just instinct. I tend to size people up pretty quickly. You've acquired a reputation for a sharp mind, not to mention sharp writing skills, as you know.

OLIVIA

I was an English major.

MEADOWS

Did you ever help Cadmus with speeches?

OLIVIA

No, sir. The truth is the former President and I had scarcely met before last week in New York, July 3. Now my whole life has changed. I've been implicated in this whole chain of events. And in unimaginable ways. I'm even part of history now. Isn't it strange? A small-town girl from Maryland.

MEADOWS

And me a small-town boy.

OLIVIA

Under such circumstances, it's perhaps best I don't work for you, sir.

MEADOWS (heartily)

You mean, being that we are both provincials!

                    OLIVIA (laughing)

That too.

                    MEADOWS (placing his elbows on the
                    desk, leaning forward)

Let me try this on you.

                    (He reads from a draft.)

"My fellow Americans, I come to you tonight with a heavy heart in the wake of one of the most tumultuous and troubling weeks in the history of our great republic. Our President and Vice- President have, as you no doubt already know, resigned, and so, through no actions of my own, but as a consequence of the procedures of succession laid out in our constitution, I speak to you tonight as your President. It is a charge I do not take lightly, especially in light of recent events."

                    (He looks up.)

                    OLIVIA

I think it sets precisely the right tone, Mr. President.

                    MEADOWS

Jim. When you are in this office, alone with me, please call me Jim, Olivia.

                    OLIVIA

Jim. I might quibble with the word "consequence," which often has negative connotations. And I wouldn't put "lightly" so close to "light."

                    MEADOWS

I quite agree. (He sips his drink, stares out the window, then turns back to the text.) Isn't it funny, print looks green after staring at the sun.

                    OLIVIA

Perhaps "result" for "consequence" would be better.

MEADOWS (adruptly standing, speaking half to himself)

You know it's hard to concentrate when there is so much news, fake or otherwise, swirling around. (More directly) I'm sorry, Olivia, but there is one thing on the news this morning I need to confirm didn't happen?

OLIVIA (taken aback)

Sir?

MEADOWS

Cadmus, even before his wife in interred, is trying to squelch rumors about the causes of her death, as you know. Can you believe his suggestion that the Deep State drove her to it?

OLIVIA

I think it's incumbent on Langford to address this, ridiculous as it is on the face of it.

MEADOWS

I've said as much to him. But I want give him some space. I don't want him to think I'm crossing any lines. We need an independent security division. Did Cadmus try to buy you off in any way? Insure your silence? As some have suggested.

OLIVIA

That's the real "Fake News" I can assure you...Jim...there's nothing to it. I haven't even spoken to the former President, nor for that matter Langford, since the night of the First Lady's passing. And to think those terrible photos by the FBI were released. Leaked.

MEADOWS

I hope to God it wasn't the FBI that leaked them. And I can't help wonder about Stuart's role.

OLIVIA

But he thought so highly of the President...Cadmus. Unless he sees some gain in it, for Cadmus. The media, we know, will stop at nothing. To see her like that draped like a slain queen over the vanity, it only goes to reinforce I think the idea that Cadmus–I'll call him that now, I guess–thought himself a king.

MEADOWS

Well, he acted as such at times, regrettably.

OLIVIA

I've been called the "King's Mistress."

MEADOWS

...Sorry, but I felt I had to ask. There can't be any secrets between us if we are to work closely together. What's holding me up in writing the speech is, more than a lack of concentration, a feeling that I lack all the necessary information related to this week's tornado of events. The country is counting on me to deliver the truth, as we know it at this time. Trust is the coin of the realm. I must put the needs of the country before anything else, including my own desires and sympathies. You understand, I hope?

OLIVIA (tearing up)

Certainly, sir. Please forgive these tears.

(Meadows looks about his desk.)

MEADOWS

Where do they keep the tissues around here?

(Meadows sits, opens a drawer, and then another, finding a box of tissues in the second.)

Ah, here.

(Hands Olivia a tissue. She leans forward, wipes away tears.)

OLIVIA

Thank you. I've been holding back tears all this week, feeling that as a Homeland Security employee, even a former one, I would need to be strong–ignore the rumors, and put aside any personal feelings I had. I was not close to President Cadmus, and even less the First Lady, but I held them both in high esteem. And even had I not, I take no pleasure in any tragic fall. I do believe there is more to come in the investigations that will further negatively impact Cadmus–though what may be revealed, I do not have direct knowledge of.

MEADOWS

Even I'm in the dark. The Justice Department has its own rules in these things. In any case, the investigations must be allowed to play out, however the chips fall–suddenly that word "Chips" seems fraught. Of course I myself did not collude in any respect with anyone, foreign or domestic, to further Cadmus's presidential prospects–in fact, I was never really in his camp–but how odd to think I wouldn't be sitting here, as President, had his opponent been elected. No one ever knows what twists and turns are ahead. To be Speaker of the House was my goal in life, my dream job. I never hankered after the Presidency. At least not consciously!

(They laugh. Reaching across the desk, he touches her hand.)

MEADOWS

I'm not married, you know.

OLIVIA (warmly)

I know.

(Meadows rises from his desk, paces, turns to rear window, and then looks again at Olivia.)

MEADOWS

I'm not sure how comfortable the nation will be with a bachelor President. I want to present them with the picture of a first family they can be proud of, and one to replace in their minds that of Cadmus, his dead wife, and their grieving son. I feel most of all for young Richie. To lose his mother, and in, as they say, such a public fashion! The rumors he's had to endure! I have no children of my own, as you certainly know. But I could at least offer the nation the picture of a new man and wife—President and First Lady—one which might help erase from their minds the events of the recent past. They didn't flinch at the fact of an older man, Cadmus, and a younger woman, Basia—poor Basia—occupying the White House...so if I were to take a wife, someone younger, likewise, I don't think the public would hold that against me. And of course occupying such a very, very demanding job, one needs all the support one can get. I'll need someone at the back of me, Olivia. Someone in my corner. Someone who knows their way around. That I can trust implicitly. Someone smart.

(He stands, walks over near to her. She looks up at him.)

OLIVIA

Are you asking me to marry you, Mr. President?

MEADOWS (he kneels)

I am, Olivia. To at least think about it. We could do great things together, for ourselves and for the country. I don't really feel comfortable living in this big house all alone. Although of course, it's only been a few days, and I might grow accustomed...

OLIVIA (rising)

Yes.

MEADOWS

"Yes?" Yes, I might grow accustomed?

OLIVIA

No. Yes, Jim, I will marry you. (Smiling) How could I say no to the President? Especially in the Oval Office. Better than a Hollywood casting couch. And further, we don't look at all alike.

(He laughs. Stands.)

MEADOWS

I hadn't thought about that. It had never occurred to me that Cadmus and Basia looked alike until...only that they were both blond. ...But we don't look alike because you are far prettier than I am!

(Just as they are about to embrace, there are three knocks on the door. Jack enters.)

JACK

A confidential missive for you, Mr. President.

MEADOWS

Thank you, Jack.

(Jack exits. Meadows lays the envelope on his desk.)

OLIVIA (nervously but firm)

Perhaps you should open it right away.

MEADOWS (holding out his pinkie finger)
Pinky promise that nothing we learn will change what we've just committed to?

(She twines her pinkie in his.)

Don't let go, while I open this. What a weight there is in being President. Already I feel it. As if each message or phone call or letter carries the weight of the world with it.

(They open the envelope together their pinkie fingers still entwined. She averts her gaze as he reads through the enclosure.)

It's about the boy. Not good news, I'm afraid. His parents can't be found after all. There was some confusion about the DNA. Makes one wonder. All but one other child, a girl, has been reunited with a parent, except if the only parent has been deported or is in jail—and quite a few are—but what bad luck—if merely bad luck it is—that this one child's parent or parents can't be found! Bad luck for him especially. But also a bad note to start off this presidency however much of the blame will fall on Cadmus first.

(They let go of each other. Meadows slumps down in his seat. Olivia remains standing. She looks out the window for a moment and then stands behind Meadows her hands on his shoulders.)

OLIVIA
I have a wild idea.

(He turns his head around and looks up at her.)

MEADOWS

Shoot.

> (She comes around, sits on the arm of his chair.)

OLIVIA

We adopt the child. I've met him, he really is a beautiful boy. And smart, I can tell. Basia really did so much in such a short time to bring him out of his traumatized condition. I'm sure she would have been happy to know that he was well taken care of. Couldn't we, Jim? It would be a great gesture. Who could object to taking care of the boy even if he is an alien?

MEADOWS

Many would object, Olivia. Even an innocent young child will not touch the hearts of many—or they will not allow it to—if he is not one of our own, if he, in their minds, doesn't belong here. It would appear to them that the President thinks he can do things that others can't. People would ask, why does this one boy get special treatment? Others might accuse us of kidnaping. Or of it being a love child.

OLIVIA (gasps, but then)

But when a president does something it is not the same as an average person doing it. Especially when he acts magnanimously, in a manly way.

MEADOWS

I don't know about that. Where did you get that notion?

OLIVIA

Cadmus's aide, Stuart. You've spoken to him?

MEADOWS

I have. A brilliant but very, very brash young man. He argues that one can achieve full consciousness only by risking everything—as he claims Cadmus did.

(He suddenly pulls her down to his lap and
kisses her.)

MEADOWS

I wonder how many kisses have taken place in the Oval Office? Or even sex!
Outside of marriage!

(She smiles, seeing an opportunity)

OLIVIA

I'll only ask this one favor, Jim. I've always wanted a child but postponed the
thought in order to concentrate on my career. This boy would be that child.

MEADOWS

Well then, your wish is granted, my dear. We will find a way to spin this to our
advantage. Stuart might be of use in that regard. Republicans are on their heels
and will be loath to hurt a new Republican president. And the Democrats are
pro lax borders, just as Cadmus said—so they too will hesitate to criticize. We will
raise this boy—what is his name?

OLIVIA

We don't know.

MEADOWS (elated, almost unhinged)

That gives us the opportunity to choose the name ourselves! We will raise him
just as if he were our own son. He will be. And the nation's First Son, so to speak.
First us getting married of course!

(They laugh. Olivia rises.)

OLIVIA

I'll leave you to your work. I'll make all arrangements for the wedding and the
boy, with your permission.

MEADOWS

I'll see to it that my Chief of Staff is informed. At the moment the public too will cut me some slack, I think. We must use both honeymoons to our advantage! But we must marry quickly. Only first a decent interval to respect the sad fate of the Cadmus family. I will meet you for dinner this evening, my dear. Here in the White House, so no one will think anything untoward, that it is anything other than a business meeting.

> (Olivia kisses him on the cheek.)

OLIVIA

Only that for now.

> (She smiles and exits. Meadows grabs his drink off the desk and turns—his back to us—to look out the back window. We see his head tilt back as he drinks.)

Scene Eight

Presidential bedroom. Early morning, the sun just poking through the curtains. Olivia, half- clothed, her hair disheveled, walks over to the vanity. She quickly looks over her shoulder back toward the bed where Meadows is asleep. She sits down. Tousles her hair.

> OLIVIA (in reference to hair)

Shit.

> (She rises and looks around the room, at last spying her purse on a chair. She gets up and walks over to the chair, then opens the purse and with her hand sorts through it, coming up empty.)

Damn.

(She sits again at the vanity, searching the top of it for a comb or brush, then pulls open the center drawer. Finds an envelope. Stares at it.)

"Confidential." Basia's DNA?

(Then opens the envelope. Looks inside. Shakes it. It is empty. She places it in a wastebasket. Closes the drawer. Staring at herself in the mirror, tousles her hair again.)

Oh, well.

(She rises, is about to return to bed, when her phone, which is also on the vanity, rings. She looks at the screen.)

Cadmus?

MEADOWS (in the bed, unseen)

Who is it, dear?

OLIVIA

It's...Cadmus, I think. Should I answer?

MEADOWS (he climbs out the bed and sits on its edge. He is in pajamas.)

How could he even think of calling you? Of course he couldn't know you were in the White House, could he?

OLIVIA (looking at the phone, which is still ringing)

It's creepy.

MEADOWS

What could he want with you?

OLIVIA

I have no idea. Comfort, perhaps. All his friends have abandoned him. People are worried what he might do. But I think his ego will protect him. And perhaps Richie—maybe Richie will look after him. Do you think he might be trying to reach you—through a safer channel? Should I say you're not...at home.

MEADOWS

Don't answer it.

(She sets down the phone on the vanity.)

OLIVIA

I'll turn off the ringer.

MEADOWS

Not likely he was trying to reach me. Though I suppose the rumor mill about us is already up and running. And I'm sure he still has his sources of information. How terrible it is, either way. And sad. Him trying to reach either of us. And how creepy, as you say—though he is unlikely to learn that he was calling his own house—or what was up to a few days ago his. Basia and Richie were about to move in entirely. Perhaps I was unwise to move in so quickly. But I wanted to reassure the nation.

OLIVIA

People understood that. Appreciated it.

MEADOWS (stands)

I see it will not be not so easy to put the Cadmus's behind us. But this afternoon the new furniture arrives at last. Langford attributed the delay to this being a crime site.

OLIVIA

Ugh. But I suppose they needed to scrub the area. (More upbeat) Even the President has to wait for his furniture to be delivered!

MEADOWS

Anyway, for us it will be a clean start. Not to mention the boy, the boy. Come back to bed, dear. I'm exhausted. We will need each other and need to be strong for the boy. We're like one of those marriage alliances made between countries for protection. Which is not to say I don't love you, Olivia. I do. When you came to me, yesterday, it was like love at first sight. But now, I've got to sleep. I'm meeting with the Cabinet at ten.

> (She sits at the vanity for a minute pondering. Then rises to go toward the bed, when her phone lights up. She stares at it for a second, wondering if she should answer.)

OLIVIA (quietly)

Jim? Honey? It's Cadmus again. What should I do?

> (She waits for his response)

My god, he's already asleep.

> (The phone lights up again. We hear her breathing. She picks up the phone. Reads.)

Oh, my god, he's texting. Stuart? It's Deep State? Can he really believe such conspiracy theories? Rumors? Heaven help us.

> (She sets the phone down on the vanity as if it is contaminated.)

(As if struck by lightening)

...My god, could Langford...? No, impossible. What would be in it for him?

(Stares into the mirror. Remains sitting at the vanity)

BLACKOUT

END OF PLAY